D1179242

Harumi's Japanese Cooking

Harumi Kurihara

First published in 2004
by Conran Octopus Limited,
a part of Octopus Publishing Group,
2–4 Heron Quays, London E14 4JP
www.conran-octopus.co.uk
Reprinted in 2005

This edition produced for The Book People Ltd,
Hall Wood Avenue, Haydock, St Helens, WA11 9UL

Recipe copyright © Harumi Kurihara
Text copyright © Harumi Kurihara and FCI London 2004
Photo copyright © Fusosha Inc.

Designed by Mark Thomson

Editor: Shirley Booth and Akiko Sakaguchi (Japan)
Text: Harumi Kurihara and Sue Hudson
Layout: Annabel Rooker
Project coordination: Sue Hudson and Akiko Sakaguchi
Translation: Tomoko Miyakoda
Photo Research: Hanako Itahashi
Special Thanks: Yutaka Seino and Naomi Ogura

Produced by International Design UK Ltd

All recipes originally published in Fusosha's
Kurihara Harumi's Suteki Recipe in Japan.

The right of Harumi Kurihara to be identified as Author
of this Work has been asserted by her in accordance
with the Copyright, Designs and Patents Act 1998

All rights reserved. No part of this work may be
reproduced, stored in a retrieval system or transmitted
in any form or by any means, electronic, electrostatic,
magnetic tape, mechanical, photocopying, recording
or otherwise, without prior permission in writing of
the publisher.

British Cataloguing-in-Publication Data
A catalogue record for this book is available
from the British Library

ISBN 1 84091 463 7
Printed and bound in China

Photo credits:
Norio Ando pp 34, 60, 61, 80, 81, 150, 151
Takeharu Hioki pp 51, 96, 97, 104, 154
Takahiro Imashimizu pp 14, 52, 53, 100, 101
Masao Kudo pp 16, 17, 27, 30, 32, 39, 45, 55, 56, 57, 68, 71–74,
76, 77, 79, 95, 114, 117, 119, 128, 132, 134, 136–138, 158, 159
Miwa Kumon pp 20, 21
Teruaki Nagamine pp 27, 35, 37, 38, 42, 44, 46, 48, 49, 64, 82,
88, 89, 106–109, 115, 139, 144, 152, 153, 155, 157, 158
Hiroyasu Nakano pp 16, 19, 22, 27, 29, 62, 125, 147, 157–159
Kazuaki Nakazato pp 13, 58, 65, 67, 85, 90, 91, 94, 98, 102, 103,
116, 120, 121, 127
Akio Takeuchi pp 5, 41, 86, 92, 110, 113, 122, 127–131, 140–143,
148, 156

Front and back cover: Akio Takeuchi
Back flap: Teruaki Nagamine

Harumi's Japanese Cooking

Harumi Kurihara

TED SMART

'Take up the challenge and enjoy
a meal with all your senses'

Contents

Foreword
Shirley Booth

To understand the cooking of Harumi Kurihara it is necessary to understand the tradition whence it comes – and from which it then, so creatively, departs. Although the underlying principles of Harumi's cooking are rooted in traditional Japanese cuisine, Harumi is a modern Japanese woman. She was born into post-war American-occupied Japan. This was a time of great change, when Japan was being pulled away from its past and its ancient traditions, towards the future – and the west. Food was a very potent symbol of this. After centuries of eating rice and fish the Japanese were now fast being introduced to bread, milk and hamburgers. Nevertheless, the Japanese love and respect for their traditional ways of eating were deep rooted and never went away.

So although Harumi's cooking is not conventional Japanese cuisine in the established sense, its sensibility underlies all she does. It is both her base and her jumping off point.

So what is this tradition? Recognising and celebrating the changing of the seasons is an important part of Japanese cuisine. In Britain we still have a few foods which we associate with the seasons – strawberries, asparagus and pumpkins, perhaps – but in Japan there are countless foods which are specifically meant to stir the senses at a particular time of year: eel in the stifling heat of summer; matsutake mushroom in autumn; bamboo shoots in spring. Furthermore, foods are not only eaten in season (frozen food has never been popular in Japan), but the way they are presented imitates the season and thereby celebrates it. For example, in autumn a dish may be garnished with 'pine needles', fashioned from deep fried noodles bound with nori sea weed, or decorated with red maple leaves. In spring, sweet cakes are fashioned into cherry blossom shapes, and dishes are adorned with sprigs of the real thing.

Using only seasonal ingredients naturally means that they will be at their freshest. And the best way to enjoy the freshest foods is to do as little as possible to them. In fact the Japanese have a saying that the best cooking is the least cooking. This is the principle behind eating sashimi, raw fish. With truly fresh fish the Japanese desire to do only one thing with it – eat it – with only a dash of soy sauce and wasabi to tease out its flavour and complement its succulence.

This is the underlying aim of all Japanese cooking techniques – to preserve and enhance the natural flavour of the ingredients. It follows then that the preparation will be simple. And what Harumi has done is to make this preparation even simpler, and to bring it into the twenty first century. This is the reason for her popularity amongst millions of modern-day Japanese women. It is also what interests us.

One of the ways that Harumi does this is in her readiness to use off-the-shelf items to make preparation quick and easy. Ready made sauces, squeezy mayonnaise, tinned tuna and spicy pastes are all pressed into service.

Another way is Harumi's willingness to harness technology and bend it to her purpose. For her carrot and tuna salad she uses the microwave to cook the carrots because she believes it helps to maintain their crispness better than by boiling them. Harumi believes in encouraging people to cook healthy and delicious food easily and, if using a microwave helps to achieve that, then that's just fine. She is, though, careful to encourage traditional techniques where she feels it makes a significant difference to a dish – she likes to make her basic stock (called dashi) from scratch, using kombu seaweed and dried fish flakes (katsuo bushi).

So, although Harumi's recipes do not entail hours spent fiddling in the kitchen making pine needles from noodles, they encompass the spirit of Japanese cooking. Where she really parts company with the traditional is in the way she enthusiastically embraces new flavours from all over the world. In the past, food in Japan tended to be either washoku – Japanese, or yoshoku – western, and each cuisine was distinct, but Harumi unselfconsciously mixes traditional Japanese ingredients with European and south east Asian new-comers. Because of the lack of grazing land for cattle in Japan, and because of Buddhist beliefs which forbade the eating of animals, dairy foods have not traditionally been a part of Japanese cuisine. Harumi though is not afraid to add cream to a dish made with miso, and she serves tofu with gorgonzola and basil. Cream cheese, tomato ketchup – they all have a role in Harumi's kitchen – and all help to make it accessible to those new to Japanese cooking.

Which leaves us with the question of what is Japanese cuisine these days?

Is it the food that's eaten in Japan? When does a food cross over from one national boundary to another? Not many people these days would question the authenticity of tomatoes in Italian and Spanish cuisine; potatoes are synonymous with Northern European cooking; and yet all were once newcomers regarded with suspicion when they were introduced from the new world. In Japan itself beef was similarly abhorred until the middle of the nineteenth century, yet sukiyaki (made with beef) is now one of the most famous Japanese dishes. In a further irony Japanese 'curry' came not from India but from England.

What most certainly does mark Harumi's food out as Japanese is the manner of its presentation. Portions are small and served separately on their own plate. Harumi does not insist that you do the same, although she'll encourage you to try, as it is part of the enjoyment of eating.

This then is stylish, unpretentious cooking that's above all eminently do-able. It's the type of food that's prepared for Japanese families, parties and restaurants: the everyday food of twenty first century Japan.

Whilst extolling the virtues of home cooked food and stylish presentation Harumi's most important message though is to enjoy what you do. Harumi certainly does – being in the kitchen with her is fun. It is this sense of fun and approachability that has made her message one that millions of Japanese women have responded to. She hopes that what she has to offer will now find a willing ear outside of Japan. I'm sure it will.

Introduction
Harumi Kurihara

I was lucky to grow up in a very traditional and beautiful part of Japan, and to have
a mother who worked in the home as well as helping with the family business.
She looked after my father and us children and she always cooked delicious fresh
Japanese food. This family background has always been my inspiration, and it is from
my mother that I learnt so many important aspects of what to cook and how to eat.
My father ran a small printing company, and my mother would cook three times

a day. She would get up at five in the morning to ensure that a hot meal was on the table for her family by six. In the evening she cooked a light meal for the employees too. Even though she no longer has to cook for so many, she still gets up early and uses the time whilst the rice is cooking to prepare the rest of the meal and get ready for the day – this is her personal time. Unlike most Japanese women these days my mother wears a kimono every day, finding it comfortable and easy to wear. I myself have inherited her habit of getting up early and I too relish the peace of early mornings, pottering in my kitchen, creating a harmonious and happy life for my family. In the past, of course, it was quite common for women to spend a lot of time in the kitchen, but these days it's a rarity.

Our home was always full of people; our family, the people working for my father, friends and visitors. My mother would quite often find herself making a meal for around a dozen people, but she always made it look easy and would quietly just get on with it – with each individual dish perfectly prepared.

My mother inspired me to see that although there are many things in life that may seem routine, or even boring, like cooking every day for your family, if you approach it with the right attitude you can achieve great satisfaction. By taking care of detail you can find happiness in small every day things, which make all the difference to a family who are living in the same house and sharing meals together.

When I look at my mother I feel such tenderness and pride. I am so impressed by her ability to carry on calmly through good times and bad.

Like many Japanese families, we lived by the sea so naturally we ate a lot of fish, but, unusually for those days, we also ate quite a lot of meat. Whatever my mother served was always carefully prepared, using ingredients that we consider important for good health, such as a variety of seaweed, sesame, soy sauce and of course rice. After all, meals cooked for your family aren't simply to fill empty stomachs, but to ensure healthy bodies too.

Now, in my own home I can see the influence of that background; the influence of my parents, and in particular my mother. I too have a home filled with family and visitors. I too rise early to get the house ready for another day , prepare food and cook for my family, to sustain them and to keep them healthy – my main drive comes from cooking for my family and friends.

In the same way I am not interested in decorating my food for the sake of it. Too many cooks these days add gratuitous decoration to their dishes, thinking that it makes the dish look more beautiful, but I don't, and I'm sure this is the reason why my books seem to have had such appeal in Japan.

My recipes and Japanese cuisine

You will find when you come to look at my recipes that I try to make meals from readily available ingredients, the type of things that people already have in their pantry or refrigerator or, indeed, using left-overs. Then I add a twist using some new seasoning, which makes it special. It has simply been the needs of my own family that have driven me to create new and interesting ways to eat familiar food. One of my most popular recipes is my carrot and tuna salad – I created this over twelve years ago and I still receive letters about it. I dressed the salad in a way which just seems to have inspired people. Another example is one of my hamburger recipes – here I added some shavings of burdock (a Japanese root vegetable called gobo) to the meat mixture, giving it a Japanese accent and at the same time adding something healthy.

Of course, the foundation of my cooking is traditional Japanese cuisine, and to learn how to cook Japanese food is to take a voyage to a culture with a different sensibility. The presentation, the variety and the seasonality all mark out Japanese food as a unique cuisine, and, although it looks simple there is complexity in the balance of the seasoning.

Many of my western friends are surprised when they hear of traditional Japanese thinking on variety in eating – we think that you should eat around thirty different types of food a day. That's why one meal contains so many different things. I think if a meal is made up of only a few ingredients it can be very boring – we need to have different flavours and even different textures to create balance and interest. It's worth noting also that this traditional way of eating has been credited with helping the Japanese people stay slim, as well as having many other health benefits.

Rice

The most important ingredient though in nearly every meal is rice. Rice is the centre of Japanese culinary life – the most important thing – the main dish.

When you go to buy rice in Japan (or in Oriental stores abroad), you'll find a bewildering array of packages and sacks, all seemingly identical but to the connoisseur all subtly different. Japanese rice is short grain and full of flavour. This type of short grain rice is easier than the long grain variety to pick up with chopsticks. I am sure that many Japanese, like myself, could not imagine life without rice.

Tableware and Presentation

Another important thing that you'll notice when looking at a Japanese meal is that it is served on lots of different plates and bowls. Most westerners visiting a Japanese house are astonished by the huge number of dishes crammed into the kitchen cupboards. There are small dishes for soy sauce, long plates for grilled fish, bowls with lids on for miso soup and so on, and, unlike western tableware, the pieces don't have to match.

In addition to ceramics we have glass, lacquer, metal and wooden dishes. In summer we use a lot of glass dishes to provide us with a visual sense of coolness – something you really need in the hot, humid Japanese summers. Lacquer is traditionally used in winter when its soft warmth is so appreciated. Those of you who are familiar with sushi will probably have seen the beautiful wooden plates that are often used to serve it on. Bamboo, which is so prevalent in Japan, is extensively and creatively used. The sheer range of materials reflect the diversity of the cuisine and emphasise the importance of presentation in Japanese meals.

Newcomers to this style of eating are often surprised by the extremely diverse range of dishes used, but I love tableware and one of my greatest pleasures in travelling is scouring antique shops, markets and department stores for unusual ceramics. Some pieces can be made of delicate high quality bone china or porcelain, while others are made from heavy earthenware, but we relish the contrast created by such a presentation.

In fact, an important part of the cook's job is choosing the best dish for each recipe, as the correct dish will complete the picture of the meal. In common with much of Japanese art, such as sumi-e (the traditional black and white brush stroke painting), we believe that simplicity is a key element in beauty. This simplicity also means that each dish holds only a small portion of food so that the dish itself can seen and appreciated. Many of my Japanese friends who travel abroad tell me how shocked they are to see a mountain of food arriving on one plate. They feel overwhelmed by the quantity and see it as almost obscene. No, we prefer to have lots of dishes holding small quantities of each individual recipe.

I divide my own huge collection of dishes into three different groups. There are the dishes that I use every day – easy to use, usually not expensive and easy to replace. Then there are what could be called the 'dolls house' dishes – tiny little plates and bowls which remind me of the small dishes that I would play with as a child. These dishes are typically Japanese and are used for soy sauce, dressings or other condiments. The final group is what I think of as my 'reward' dishes. These are plates or bowls that are usually unique and sometimes expensive. I consider that I work hard every day and so occasionally I like to reward myself by indulging my love of beautiful things. Using one of these 'reward' dishes makes a meal feel extra special.

I think in the west many people buy themselves one set of matching china and never change it or add to it, despite the inevitable changes in taste and fashion that we experience as an individual and as a society. Over the years my tastes have changed and I enjoy buying new items to use for our meals. At the moment I am using a lot

of oval shaped dishes as I think they are versatile and attractive for many different types of foods.

In fact, I encourage you to experiment with different shapes – I would become so bored if I could use only round plates. Also experiment with how you use dishes – there is no reason why you shouldn't use them for candles or flowers at a party. Although traditionally we used to say that certain plates must be used for this and another for that I am feeling increasingly liberated from that way of thinking. I think you should use a variety of different tableware at any one time and not be limited too much by the traditional seasonality of tableware. Use your imagination and have fun! I think it is a fantastic way of tapping into your own creativity.

Etiquette

Traditionally in Japan we were encouraged not to talk whilst eating. Some of you may have seen samurai films with each warrior sitting in front of his own little table, separate from the others. I suppose it was almost like a form of meditation – eating silently. In contrast, if you've ever visited a Japanese bar or pub, where customers are busy eating a variety of dishes (otsumami) with their drinks, you'll have noticed that silence is definitely not on the menu. In fact you'll have noticed how busy it is, with everyone rushing around and customers chatting noisily.

Japanese eating habits then are changing – as are the habits of people all around the world. We are no longer closed off to influences from the rest of the world – in fact I think that we are embracing different cuisines, ingredients and flavours with great enthusiasm. The recipes in this book reflect that experience. However, I think that even when we adopt another country's taste we subtly alter it to suit our own, and in the process we are creating a new Japanese cuisine.

Nevertheless, there are three important principles in the Japanese style of eating which remain unchanged, and which I believe mark out our cuisine as different. These are variety, seasonality and presentation.

I hope that when you use the recipes in this book you will also start looking more closely at how you serve up your food, and also when to serve particular foods. Wherever possible try to eat seasonally and use visual reminders of the season with the food. In Japanese ceramics you can easily find plates with images of red maple leaves on,

reminders of autumn, but if these are not available then maybe use a leaf or something from the garden, or a plate with autumnal colour running through it.

I have designed the book so you can start by choosing a particular dish, and then serving it either as a starter or as a main course. I think you will be amazed at how easy it is to do and how different the meal experience is from what you are used to. A lot of small dishes with different flavours make a very exciting way of eating. I hope you will also notice how healthy such meals are. It is generally accepted that Japanese food is healthy and this is mainly because it aims to satisfy our needs through variety rather than quantity. However, Japanese tastes are changing, and these days it's common to find desserts using dairy products. To reflect this I have included some non-traditional desserts in my book.

I hope that you will enjoy these recipes – they were all originally published in my 'Suteki Recipe' magazine and proved to be very popular. I have tried to select ones that can be easily tackled outside of Japan, relying mainly on ingredients which most of you will have in your kitchen already. There are, however, a few which are more challenging, for those of you who already know Japanese cuisine.

I hope that you will enjoy trying a new way of presenting food, of eating food, and of using tableware. But most of all I hope that attention to such things will bring you the joy and satisfaction that my mother taught me through her own example. We all know that life can be difficult and hard but the challenge is in trying to live it well. I strongly believe that we can enhance our lives by taking another look at how we eat.

So take up the challenge and enjoy a meal with all your senses – Japanese food is not frightening, just exciting and delicious!

How to Use This Book

The idea of this book is to introduce Japanese contemporary home cooking to readers around the world. It is hoped that it will demystify the cuisine and encourage people who are interested to try a new style of cooking and eating.

It is not my aim to require you, the reader, to go out and hunt down lots of obscure ingredients. I have tried to select recipes, wherever possible, that can be made fairly easily wherever you are in the world. Ingredients, even vegetables, are slightly different from country to country, so I ask you to use your common sense and to read the ingredients notes and glossary.

I have included suggestions for substitution of ingredients but I would encourage you to try these recipes even if you can't find everything needed; in most cases you will be able to achieve a result which is close to the original recipe. If you have never had Japanese food before, I would recommend that you start with the easier recipes and build up confidence and knowledge of the look and flavour of this food.

Just remember the concepts I talked about in my introduction; variety, presentation and seasonality. You can even take non-Japanese dishes and create the feel of a Japanese meal with them if you remember these principles.

Nevertheless, there are certain flavours that differ from other cuisines, which require some understanding and an open mind. One of the most obvious differences is that of sweetness: it is very common to use sugar in the preparation of a savoury dish. Mirin, another important ingredient, is quite sweet and frequently used. To people who do not know Japanese food, this comes as a surprise. I believe that this sweetness balances the meal – it means we do not necessarily have strong cravings for desserts or sweets. It also balances out the saltiness of the soy sauce, miso and dashi. Try the recipes with the sugar but reduce it if it is really not to your taste.

There is also quite a saltiness to Japanese food, mainly due to soy sauce. Again, try it with the full amount of soy sauce and reduce if you really want to.

Underlying many of the recipes are the flavours of dashi, mirin and soy sauce, in various combination.

Dashi is a fish stock made with kombu seaweed and dried fish flakes (katsuo bushi). It is easy to make (see page 27), if you can get the ingredients. If you cannot find them then use a light fish stock (adding a little chicken stock if you like). You can even make it by simply boiling a piece of white fish in water. Although it is light its characteristic flavour is one worth aiming for.

Mirin is harder to substitute. It is a type of sweetened alcohol and is usually used only in cooking. It adds a great mellow, soft sweetness. Some books say you can replace it with a little extra sugar but I think that it really is worth trying to track down.

Soy sauce is now quite easy to find outside of Japan – use Japanese dark soy sauce, unless the recipe specifies light soy sauce. I think it is worth trying to find a good Japanese soy sauce as it is subtly different from the Chinese brands.

Then there is the question of herbs and spices. You should be able to find quite a lot of these items in Asian supermarkets. If you can't, try the substitutions that I have suggested. There are many recipes that need sesame paste. Tahini (a Greek sesame paste) or even unsweetened peanut butter, can be used as a substitute. However, again I would urge you to spend money on Japanese sesame paste as it is made from toasted sesame seeds and is very distinctive in its rich creaminess.

In many of my recipes you will find references to granulated chicken stock and potato starch. They are both frequently used ingredients but, if you go to a Japanese food shop, you might like to buy the original Japanese items. Torigara soup powder is what you should ask for, which is Chinese granulated chicken stock (and please note that this is different from Chinese soup paste for which I suggest you substitute a mix of chicken and beef stock). The potato starch is called katakuriko.

In addition to new flavours or combinations of flavours, you will find that there are some different styles of cooking. You will notice that I am quite relaxed about the substitution of various ingredients but I do feel strongly about the way in which vegetables are prepared for these recipes. I believe that vegetables have a very different effect on a recipe depending on how they are cut. Follow the instructions for cutting and look at the photos to replicate the look.

For all the recipes you should use really sharp knives, but especially when you are cutting raw fish. You will probably need to cultivate a good fishmonger for any of the recipes using raw fish. You should also try to master using cooking chopsticks – I think you will be amazed at just how easy they make cooking, especially any dish that's made in a wok.

As I created many of my recipes for busy people, I often include cooking instructions that feature the microwave. If you do not have one, cook the ingredients in a way that you are familiar and comfortable with. I have found, like so many Japanese, that the microwave, if used judiciously, is a great aid in the kitchen.

While I like to use modern technology, I also feel it is important to use your hands for mixing; you will get a better result if you do so. You may also find it helpful to have a few small mixing bowls ready before you start cooking – many of my recipes require you to prepare marinades, sauces or mixing ingredients at an early stage of preparation.

Quite a few recipes require you to use a lid which is placed directly on top of the food whilst simmering. It helps to intensify the flavours of the food being cooked and stops it moving about. If you don't have a drop lid use a circle of aluminium foil instead – just make sure it fits inside the saucepan.

For measurements, I have used the following:
1 Cup (a Japanese cup = 200ml)
1 Tablespoon = 15ml
1 Teaspoon = 5ml

Finally, remember the importance of variety, presentation and seasonality when deciding which recipes to cook. Endeavour to find a balance between the flavours of the different dishes. Above all, relax and enjoy the journey into the exciting world of Japanese cuisine.

Dashi

At the heart of many Japanese dishes is a fish based stock called dashi. In Japan many people use instant dashi but I find this too salty and much prefer to make my own. You can subtly alter the flavour by the length of time you boil it. If you can get the ingredients it is really worth experimenting with. Good dashi can provide you with the most fantastic base, one that can transform a recipe from being just good to being fantastic.

kombu seaweed

dried fish flakes

Ingredients for 4 cups/800ml dashi:
5 cups/1 litre water
10cm square piece of dried kombu seaweed
30g dried fish flakes (katsuo bushi – shavings from a piece of dried bonito/tuna fish)

1 Wipe a piece of kombu seaweed with a damp cloth and then soak it in a pan with the 5 cups/1 litre of water. I usually leave the kombu seaweed for 10 minutes.

2 Heat the water and when it is getting warm take out the piece of kombu seaweed. As the water comes to the boil add the fish flakes and cook for one or two minutes on a high heat, then turn it off. It is ready to be strained when the flakes have sunk to the bottom of the pan. These flakes are sometimes re-used for a weaker version of dashi. You can freeze any unused dashi stock.

Appetisers & Entrées

When you order a drink in a bar in Japan you will always receive a small dish of food to accompany the drink – called otsumami, it's like tapas in Spain. In our family we like to do the same – to nibble on small dishes while we drink and chat, when we get together as a family at the end of a busy working day to catch up with each other's news.

Everyone in my family enjoys cooking, so we all take part in preparing a wide range of starters for us to nibble on whilst drinking and chatting. Sometimes we may have up to eight different appetisers – cooked by different members of the family. We each have our specialities – my husband likes cooking western style dishes, whilst my daughter prefers experimenting with ethnic and Italian. My son, on the other hand, is a traditionalist and likes to cook Japanese dishes. In any case we always enjoy the relaxed informal atmosphere and having time to eat appetisers in an unhurried way.

Many of these dishes can be served as appetisers to accompany drinks or as part of a main meal as an entrée – it is up to you to decide how you want serve them.

Scallop Sauté with Miso Sauce
Hotate no Sauté Miso Sauce

These scallops make a good starter or they can be served as part of a larger Japanese-style meal. I think that the combination of Japanese flavours, such as miso, and the western flavour of Parmesan cheese makes for a delicious and exciting dish.

(Serves 4)
240g very fresh scallops (without their coral)
salt and pepper
8g crushed garlic (1 clove)
plain flour – to dust the scallops
1–2 tablespoons sunflower or vegetable oil
2 tablespoons white wine
2 tablespoons miso
1 tablespoon mirin
1 teaspoon soy sauce
1 teaspoon caster sugar
1–2 tablespoons water
½ tablespoon grain mustard
2 tablespoons double cream
small bunch of watercress
freshly grated Parmesan cheese – to taste

1 Season the scallops with the salt, pepper and garlic and then lightly dust with flour.

2 Heat the oil in a small frying pan. Briefly fry both sides of the scallops until sealed on the outside, but still rare in the middle.

3 Take the pan off the heat and remove the scallops. Add the white wine and then the miso, mirin, soy sauce, sugar and water to the pan and stir. Return to the heat and bring to the boil, stirring, then remove. Mix in the grain mustard and double cream.

4 Tear the leaves off the watercress and arrange on a large plate. Chop the stems finely and set aside as a garnish. Place the scallops on the bed of watercress leaves, pour the hot sauce over and garnish with the finely chopped watercress stems. Sprinkle with Parmesan cheese and serve.

White Fish Salad

This makes a great starter or a light lunch. I like using a firm white fish like sea bream for this recipe (you could use cod or haddock).

(Serves 4)
100g–150g sashimi-quality white fish fillets
salt and pepper
a little crushed garlic – to taste
½ tablespoon sunflower or vegetable oil
1 packet of mixed green salad leaves

Sesame Dressing:
3 tablespoons sesame paste
2 tablespoons hot water
a little granulated chicken stock powder
1 tablespoon caster sugar
1 tablespoon soy sauce
1 tablespoon rice vinegar
½ tablespoon mirin
½ teaspoon red chilli paste or to-ban-jan

2 tablespoons coarsely ground sesame seeds
a little finely chopped spring onion or chives –
   to garnish
some coarsely ground black pepper

Ingredients Note:
If you cannot find good quality Japanese sesame paste then use tahini (Greek sesame paste) or even unsweetened peanut butter. The final dressing should be moderately thick.

1 Season the fish with the salt, pepper and garlic. In a frying pan heat the oil to medium and pan fry both sides of the fish until it is lightly cooked but crispy on the outside. Let the fish cool and then slice diagonally into bite size pieces.
2 Tear the salad leaves, wash and drain.
3 Mix the ingredients for the sesame dressing – mixing in the order listed above but without the sesame seeds. When combined, mix in the sesame seeds.
4 Arrange the salad leaves on a plate, place the sliced fish fillet on top and dress with the sesame sauce. Garnish with the chopped spring onion and freshly ground black pepper.

Steamed Asari Clams with Ponzu Soy Sauce

I suppose that this recipe is Japan's answer to the famous French recipe for mussels in a white wine sauce. There is something very special about being presented with a bowl of steaming hot clams, still in their shells, and the citric fragrance from the ponzu soy sauce (see page 80) makes it a truly memorable experience.

(Serves 4)
400–500g asari clams (still in their shell)
¾ cup/150ml ponzu soy sauce (see page 80)
roughly chopped shiso leaves or a mix
    of fresh mint and basil – to garnish
toasted white sesame seeds – to taste

1 To clean the clams, leave in salt water overnight – the water should be of the same saltiness as seawater; they will open their shells allowing the beards and sand to be removed easily. Take out any dead clams, wash well and then rub the shells together. Drain well.
2 Put a wok onto a medium heat. Add the clams and the ponzu soy sauce, cover with a lid and let the clams steam. When the shells open, pour the clams and sauce into a serving bowl. Sprinkle with shiso leaves and the toasted sesame seeds. Eat while hot.

Soy Egg Appetizers
Shoyu Tamago no Zensai

I love appetizers and party food. As well as enjoying choosing the tastes and colours of the food itself, I take great delight in deciding on which plates to display it. These eggs are just so simple to prepare but stunning to look at, with different coloured toppings. You can experiment with other ideas, such as pickles, olives and cress. I happen to love any kind of egg cooking, but this is one of my favourites.

(Serves 4)
6–8 small hard-boiled eggs
1 tablespoon rice vinegar
2 tablespoons soy sauce
1 teaspoon caster sugar

Suggested Toppings:
salmon roe
cream cheese
olives
cress
pickles

1   Shell the eggs. Mix the vinegar, soy sauce and sugar together, making sure the sugar dissolves. Put the eggs with the marinade into a large plastic bag. Leave to marinate for 2–3 hours, moving the eggs around in the bag from time to time to ensure an even colour.

2   Remove the eggs from the bag and cut them in half lengthways. Place on a serving dish and decorate the yolk with a teaspoon of salmon roe, cream cheese or any other topping you choose. Serve as finger food or with salad leaves as a starter.

Chinese Style Dumplings
Gyoza

These are often served alongside Chinese style noodles (Ramen – see page 46) but I think they are also great for parties, barbeques or buffet meals. You can find many different recipes for dumplings but this is one of the easiest.

3 dumplings per person (Serves 4)
200g uncooked prawns
100g minced pork
1 tablespoon sake
½ teaspoon salt
a pinch of sugar and pepper
1 teaspoon finely chopped ginger
2 tablespoons liquid chicken stock
1 teaspoon potato starch or cornflour
50g finely chopped Chinese chives (Niva)
2 tablespoons sesame oil
12 thin round pastry skins (you can find these in most Chinese supermarkets)
1½ tablespoons sunflower or vegetable oil
¼ cup/50ml hot water
For the dipping sauce: rice vinegar and soy sauce with a few drops of chilli oil (La-Yu)

Ingredients Note:
You should be able to find the more unusual ingredients for this recipe in Chinese supermarkets. If you can't find nira, use finely chopped spring onion and 1 large clove of garlic, finely chopped. Also note that the pastry skins used here are round, not rectangular.

1 First de-vein the prawns by bending and, using a toothpick, pull out the dark vein. Then, with a knife, mince half of the prawns finely and cut the rest into larger 1cm square pieces.

2 Put the prawns and minced pork into a large bowl and mix well. Add the sake, salt, sugar, pepper, grated ginger and stock and mix together, finally adding the flour bit by bit until you have a fairly firm paste.

3 Add the Chinese chives and half the sesame oil – this will give the mixture an appealing nutty aroma and taste.

4 Divide the mixture into 12 and shape each portion into a short sausage shape. Put each 'sausage' into the centre of each pastry skin and fold over.

5 Pour the sunflower oil into a large frying pan and place on a medium heat. Arrange the dumplings in rows and fry until crispy and brown on one side.

6 Turn them over and cook for a short time and then throw in the hot water, covering with a lid as quickly as you can to keep the steam in. Leave them to steam until cooked (about 5 minutes).

7 When most of the liquid is gone, uncover, pour the remaining tablespoon of sesame oil on top, and cook until crispy again. If you have a problem with the dumplings sticking to the bottom of the pan, then try wiping the bottom of the pan underneath with a damp cloth – they should come loose. Serve immediately, with a dipping sauce of vinegar, soy sauce, and chilli oil – delicious!

Tuna Tartare

I got the inspiration for this recipe from a restaurant in New York. Enjoy the marriage of Japanese taste and western presentation.

(Serves 4)
1 tablespoon dashi stock or fish stock
1 tablespoon light soy sauce
1 tablespoon olive oil
½ tablespoon rice vinegar (or you can
   use lemon juice or wine vinegar instead)
a little mustard
200g fresh sashimi-quality tuna
4 shiso leaves or a mix of fresh mint and basil
wasabi – to taste
1 tablespoon chopped spring onions or chives
grated ginger – to taste
1 tablespoon finely chopped onion
a little finely chopped garlic
a little coarsely ground pepper

1 Mix together the dashi, soy sauce, olive oil, vinegar and mustard in a bowl and set aside to use as a dressing when serving up.

2 Finely chop the tuna fillets and shred the shiso leaves.

3 Divide the chopped tuna into three and mix one part with shiso leaves, another with the spring onions or chives and the third with the finely chopped onions and garlic.

4 Make 4 tuna balls out of each bowl of tuna mix. Dress the shiso leaf-flavoured balls with a dab of wasabi. Dress the spring onion-flavoured ones with a dab of grated ginger, and the onion and garlic balls with freshly ground pepper.

5 Serve one ball of each flavour and then pour over the dressing just before eating.

Asparagus with Crab Mayonnaise Dressing

Asparagus and crab are both very popular ingredients in Japan. We mainly use the white meat from the long legged Alaskan crab but try this with whatever crab is local to you. I like my asparagus only just cooked – so it still has a bite to it. Try it this way and you will find it is so much tastier and more satisfying than when it's soft.

(Serves 4)
500g fresh green asparagus
150g white crab meat
1 tablespoon white wine
½ cup/100ml (or 85g) mayonnaise
salt and pepper

1   Prepare the asparagus by discarding the woody ends and side leaves then boil until just cooked (about 3–5 minutes depending on thickness). Be careful not to allow the tips to become overcooked. Remove and cool by placing the asparagus into a bowl of iced water.
2   Roughly flake the crabmeat into a medium size bowl. Sprinkle with the white wine and then mix in the mayonnaise, salt and pepper. If the dressing seems a bit stiff add a little milk – you need a soft runny consistency.
3   Drain the asparagus and pat dry. Cut it into smaller lengths, suitable for the size of the plates you are planning to use. If there are any small pieces of asparagus that you are not putting on the plate then chop them finely and add them to the sauce. Arrange the asparagus on four individual plates and pour the crab mayonnaise over.

Soup & Noodles

We love soup! A Japanese meal needs soup – served and enjoyed at the same time as everything else. I find the western tradition of having soup at the beginning leaves me too full to enjoy the rest of the meal.

The most typical Japanese soup is misoshiru (miso soup – made with miso paste). Traditionally, it was served at every meal, but especially with breakfast. These days, although many families no longer eat a traditional breakfast, they often have miso soup with their lunch or dinner.

Miso soup is one of the best examples of how Japanese food changes according to the seasons. Although the basic soup doesn't change, the vegetables which it contains reflect the season – for example bamboo shoots in spring, aubergines in summer, mushrooms in autumn and sweet potato in winter. Soup is one of the best ways in Japanese cuisine where a large variety of seasonal ingredients can be enjoyed as a natural part of the diet.

After the Second World War, the American influence brought with it the fashion for thicker chowder and cream soups, and even now I think Japan is one of the few places outside America where you can easily find cream of corn soup. More recently however, Asian tastes like Hot and Sour Soup are gaining popularity, especially with young Japanese, like my daughter, who love the spicier foods of south east Asia.

There are many indigenous noodles in Japan; soba, somen and udon to name a few. We enjoy eating these noodles hot or cold, often with quite noisy gusto. But we have also adopted noodles from around the world, in particular pasta. I believe that our experience with the delicate Japanese noodles has enabled us to cook pasta in the correct 'al dente' way. You won't find soggy pasta in any of the many Italian restaurants in Japan! What you will find is that many of these restaurants have adapted pasta to the Japanese taste, serving it with ingredients, like shiitake mushrooms and nori, not used in its native Italy.

Seafood Miso Soup

Clams are very popular in Japan, especially these small asari clams. I think they make a fantastic addition to this simple miso soup. You can make the soup even tastier by using seasonal flavours such as the leaves of the sansho plant (kinome) in spring, ginger in the summer and yuzu (a Japanese citrus fruit) in autumn and winter. It is not always easy to find kinome leaves outside Japan but use them if you can. They have a taste that makes me feel glad to have been born in Japan. If you can't find them, then experiment with chives, spring onions, flat leaf parsley or coriander.

In this recipe I suggest using the heads of uncooked prawns as a garnish – they look stunning and add extra taste – but don't waste the rest of the prawns. Use them for one of the many recipes in this book that uses prawns, like the Chinese dumpling recipe (Gyoza see page 36).

(Serves 4)
300g asari clams (or any other type of baby clam still in its shell)
30g wakame seaweed
150–200g pak choy
herbs such as kinome – to taste
4 cups/800 ml water
1 chicken stock cube or 2 teaspoons granualted chicken stock powder
4 uncooked prawn heads
2 tablespoons miso

Ingredients Note:
Seaweed is really good for you and increasingly available in large supermarkets. However, if you cannot find any then try a little spinach instead.

1 Clean the clams and leave them in salted water overnight; the salted water should be similar to seawater in saltiness. When you are ready to make the soup, rinse the clams and leave them to soak for a while in unsalted water so they are ready for cooking.
2 Soak the wakame seaweed in water to remove salt, drain, squeeze and cut into bite size pieces. Chop the pak choy into 2cm wide pieces and roughly chop up the herbs.
3 Put the water in a pan and bring to the boil. Add the stock cube and let it dissolve. Then add the asari clams and the prawn heads.
4 When the clams open (this should only take a few minutes), add the miso, wakame seaweed and pak choy. Bring it all back to the boil for a short time to ensure the miso dissolves before turning off the heat.
5 Divide between 4 bowls, ensuring that each serving contains a prawn head. Sprinkle with the chopped herbs.

Spinach Noodle Soup
Horenso to Harusame Soup

These thin, light harusame noodles work really well in soups but if you cannot find them then try the thin Thai style rice noodles instead. In keeping with the transparent nature of the noodles, I like to try to keep this soup looking as clear as possible by using ingredients which will not discolour the soup. Try to use white pepper and light soy sauce as it all helps to keep this looking good.

(Serves 4)
30g uncooked harusame noodles
    or thin rice noodles
300g fresh spinach
4 cups/800ml water
1 tablespoon granulated chicken stock
    or 1½ chicken stock cube
1 tablespoon sake
salt and white pepper – to taste
light soy sauce – to taste
1 tablespoon sesame oil
chilli oil or la yu – to taste

Ingredients Note:
We often use a strongly-flavoured chilli oil called la yu – a couple of drops in this soup will work magic.

1   In a large pan of boiling water, boil the noodles, taking care not to overcook them. Drain and then cut them into easy to eat lengths.
2   Briefly boil the spinach and then soak in chilled water – this helps to keep its colour. Drain well and chop roughly into 2cm lengths.
3   Bring the 4 cups of water to the boil and add the stock and sake, then the noodles and spinach. Season with salt, white pepper and light soy sauce and finally the sesame oil, which will give it an enticing aroma.
4   Chilli oil can be added when the soup is served in bowls.

Egg Drop Soup
Kaki Tamago Jiru

This soup looks beautiful with its delicate yellow ribbons of egg and green herbs. It should be served and eaten whilst it is still very hot.

(Serves 4)
just under 4 cups/760ml dashi stock or fish stock
1 tablespoon light soy sauce
½ tablespoon soy sauce
1 tablespoon mirin
salt
2 teaspoons water mixed with 1 teaspoon potato starch or cornflour
2 eggs
chopped fresh green herbs such as mitsuba or spring onions or even lightly cooked green beans

Ingredients Note:
As this is a consommé type soup it is worth trying to find the ingredients to make the dashi from scratch, as it will provide a more delicate flavour than just shop-bought fish stock. If you do use a shop bought stock it may be rather salty so be careful when seasoning.

1　Warm the dashi or fish stock in a pan. Once it has come to the boil, add the mirin and soy sauce then gently thicken with the potato starch.

2　In a separate bowl lightly beat the eggs and add to the heated stock. Simmer for a few minutes, making sure not to overcook the eggs. Turn off the heat, pour into individual bowls, dress with herbs or green beans and serve immediately.

Chinese Style Soup Noodles
Ramen

Originating in China, ramen is a Chinese soup noodle dish which we have taken and fully adapted to our taste. Once you have the basic stock and noodles you can add a variety of toppings. We have many ramen restaurants – some are so small they only have a counter big enough for 6 people to sit at. Ramen is a favourite meal for busy office workers and impoverished students as it is quick, cheap and filling. Once you have finished the noodles and the other solid ingredients, don't be afraid to pick up the bowl and drink the remaining soup – it's not considered rude. You can even make slurping noises while eating the noodles and again it is not thought of as bad mannered!

(Serves 4)
10 cups/2 litres water
4 tablespoons granulated chicken stock
    or 6 stock cubes
½ cup/100ml pork stock (see recipe page 47)
4 tablespoons soy sauce
2 teaspoons kombu cha powder
salt – to taste
600g thin Chinese egg noodles – uncooked
chopped spring onions – to taste
menma bamboo shoots – to taste
   (see Ingredients Note)
coarsely ground black pepper
red chilli shochu – optional
sliced simmered pork and hard boiled eggs –
    optional (see opposite)

Ingredients Note:
It is worth making your own pork stock for this by simmering pork as it adds real depth of flavour. If any of you are film buffs you might recall in the Japanese film 'Tampopo' the search for the perfect soup for ramen. If you haven't seen the film it is worth tracking down – it will give you great insight into the making of ramen. If you cannot find kombu cha powder it can be omitted. Menma are preserved bamboo shoots that are used a lot in Chinese dishes.

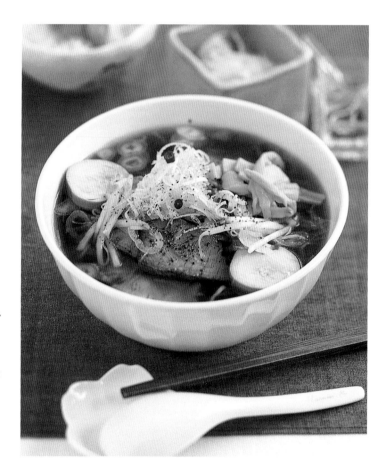

1 Make the soup. In a large pan bring the water to a boil
and add the chicken stock, pork stock, soy sauce, kombu cha
powder and salt. Bring to the boil again then turn the heat
down to the lowest possible heat and prepare the noodles.
2 In a separate pan bring a large quantity of water to the
boil and add the noodles. Cook until al dente, then drain.
3 Divide the noodles between four large warmed bowls
and ladle in the soup. Sprinkle some chopped spring onion
and the menma on top along with some sliced pork (if using).
Add pepper and chilli shochu, to taste.

Presentation Note:
Ramen is considered almost a complete meal,
so it's usually served up in large, deep bowls –
big enough to hold half a litre of liquid per person.
However, if you do not have bowls big enough
then you'll have to serve smaller amounts in
regular soup bowls. As an accompaniment
we often serve gyoza, another Chinese import,
alongside these noodles. (see page 36)

Simmered Pork

Not only does this give us a wonderful pork
stock but you can use the pork and eggs on top
of the ramen. Move the pork and eggs around
from time to time to give them an even colour.

(Serves 4)
a little sunflower or vegetable oil
500g pork loin
the green part of 1 spring onion
3cm piece ginger, peeled and crushed
½ cup/100ml soy sauce
¼ cup/50ml sake
1 tablespoon caster sugar
water
4 hard-boiled eggs (shelled)

1 Heat the oil in a saucepan to a medium heat,
add the pork and seal evenly on all sides.
2 Wipe off any excess oil from the pan (you can
do this with kitchen paper – try holding some
with cooking chopsticks). Add the spring onion,
ginger, soy sauce, sake and sugar. Pour in enough
water to almost cover the pork and increase the
heat. Once it comes to the boil, turn the heat down
to medium, skim the surface to remove any scum
and simmer for 40 minutes. During this time turn
the pork a couple of times and keep removing
any scum.
3 When the water has reduced by half, add the
eggs to the pan with the pork. Move them around
from time to time to ensure an even colour.
4 When the water has reduced to about 100ml
(around half a cup), turn off the heat and leave
to cool, then slice the pork and cut the eggs in half.
Use the stock to make the ramen and put the meat
and eggs on top.

Sesame Miso Soup with Tofu

Although young Japanese increasingly begin the day by eating western style breakfast, It is hard to imagine my parents serving anything other than a traditional one, which always includes home-made miso soup. This sesame soup recipe is a tasty variation on that theme. Miso and sesame are a very good combination and you don't need many ingredients to make this rich and delicious soup. I quite often use ready-made sesame paste but my mother prefers to stick to the traditional way and grinds her own paste from toasted sesame seeds. The aroma from the soup is amazing and drinking it seems to make your sleepiness disappear, waking you up and giving you strength for the day ahead.

1 If you are not using sesame paste, start by roasting the sesame seeds. Be careful not to burn the seeds, taking the pan off the heat once the seeds start to pop.

2 In a pestle and mortar, grind them to a sticky paste. It should smell wonderfully nutty as the seeds give off their aroma. Transfer the paste into a large mixing bowl.

3 Pour the dashi or fish stock into a pan on a moderate heat. Just before it comes to the boil add the miso paste, stirring until it dissolves. Bring to a gentle boil, slowly mix in the sesame paste and add the tofu, breaking it up into bite size pieces with your hands.

4 Serve immediately, garnished with a little chopped spring onion and a little ground sesame according to taste. You can also add seasonal cooked vegetables if you like.

(Serves 4)
100g sesame seeds or 4–5 tablespoons
   sesame paste
4 cups/800ml dashi or fish stock
300g soft/silken tofu (1 pack)
4 tablespoons miso paste

Ingredients Note:
I prefer to use the soft/silken tofu here but you can use the firm type if you prefer. The idea of breaking the tofu into small pieces with your hands comes from a Chinese style of Buddhist vegetarian cooking called Hucha Ryori. In Japan we have a traditional style of vegetarian cooking called Shojin Ryori – again based on Buddhist principles.

Pan Fried Noodles with Pork and Pak Choy
Yakisoba

This meal is ideal when you have only one packet of Chinese noodles left. You can substitute beef, chicken or any minced meat for the pork and it still tastes great. Just make sure that it is served up as quickly as possible – noodles should always be eaten piping hot. This is also a great recipe to try using cooking chopsticks, which are longer than the ones used to eat with. They are an essential part of any Japanese cook's equipment, and are particularly useful for quick stir frying.

(Serves 2)
15g fresh ginger (peeled)
150–160g pak choy
100g pork (most cuts will do)
salt and pepper
1½ cups/300ml hot water
1 teaspoon Chinese soup paste or a mix
    of chicken and beef stock
1 tablespoon soy sauce
1 tablespoon shokoshu
1 teaspoon oyster sauce
2 tablespoons sunflower or vegetable oil
150g cooked Chinese noodles
1½ tablespoons potato starch paste mixed
    with 1½ tablespoons water
1 tablespoon sesame oil
rice vinegar and mustard – to taste

1 Crush the ginger using the blade of a knife. Chop the pak choy stems into 5–6 cm juliennes and keep separate. Season the pork with salt and pepper and cut it into small strips.

2 Mix the hot water, soup paste/stock, soy sauce, shokoshu and oyster sauce in a bowl to use as a sauce later.

3 Heat a tablespoon of the sunflower oil in a wok on a medium heat. Loosen the Chinese noodles, add to the frying pan, pressing them into the bottom. When they are crispy, turn them over and cook on the other side. This is done to make them crunchy. Separate them again and then put them on a warm plate.

4 Pour a little more oil into the wok, add the ginger and fry. When you can smell its aroma, then add the pork and press it down.

5 Next, add the pak choy stems and after 1 minute add the leaves. Stir in the sauce you made earlier.

6 Bring to a simmer and add the potato starch, thickening to taste. Add the sesame oil for an extra special aroma.

7 Remove the piece of ginger and pour the sauce over the noodles. Add vinegar and Japanese mustard to taste.

Japanese Somen Noodle Salad

When I asked my husband which of my recipes he liked the best, he immediately answered, 'Somen salad!' You can cook this simple dish using ingredients that you probably already have in your cupboard. If you do not have these noodles you can use something else like spaghettini. It is a very versatile salad that can be used to accompany many meals – it also works well in lunchboxes.

(Serves 2–3)
100g somen noodles
90g tinned tuna (or ham, if you prefer)
50g onion
100g cucumber
4 tablespoons mayonnaise
a little salt, pepper, and soy sauce

Ingredients Note:
Cucumbers in Japan are small – which means they are less watery than large ones. Try to get small cucumbers, but if you can't then use a large one and scoop out the seeds from the middle.

1 Fill a large pan with plenty of water and bring to the boil. Add the noodles to the pan and cook until al dente. When cooked, rinse under cold running water, ensuring that the noodles are all separated, then drain well.
2 Drain the tuna. Cut the onion thinly into half moons and soak in water for about 5–10 minutes to take away any sharpness. Drain the onions and squeeze to remove any excess water. Finely slice the cucumber and season with salt. Leave for 5–10 minutes then squeeze to remove any excess water.
3 Mix the noodles, tuna, onion, cucumber and mayonnaise in a bowl and season with salt, pepper, and soy sauce.

Spaghettini with Fish Roe Dressing
Mentaiko Spaghettini

This is one of the most popular types of pasta in Japan and is a great example of how a foreign ingredient has been adapted to Japanese taste. I think you will find it quite an eye opener.

(Serves 2)
160g uncooked spaghettini
80–100g mentaiko (see Ingredients Note)
28g butter
nori seaweed – to taste
shiso leaves or fresh basil and mint leaves – to taste
chopped spring onion or chives – to garnish
½ teaspoon kombu cha powder
soy sauce – to season

Ingredients Note:
Mentaiko is quite difficult to substitute. Its unique taste comes from the salting process and chilli. Kombu cha powder may also be hard to substitute, but you can make something similar with a little strong fish stock.

1 Boil the spaghettini in a pan of salted water until al dente.
2 Soften the butter and beat until creamy. Remove the thin membrane from the mentaiko and mix the roe with the butter.
3 Finely shred the dried seaweed and the shiso leaves.
4 When the spaghettini is cooked, drain well. Immediately mix with the mentaiko and the butter and season with kombu cha powder and soy sauce.
5 Put onto a serving plate, sprinkle the dried seaweed and shiso leaves on top and garnish with spring onions or chives.

Rice

I cannot live without rice, and I think many Japanese people feel the same. Like other Asians we just love rice. In fact I could eat rice three times a day, but I certainly have to have it at least once a day. The rice we use in Japan is short grained, which becomes sticky when cooked – this makes it easier to eat with chopsticks. We never use the long grain 'fluffy' rice. At the risk of sounding a little nationalistic I think that Japanese rice is the best in the world.

As it is such an important element in a Japanese meal it is worth trying different varieties to find the one that suits you the best. I continually try rice from different regions of Japan as different regions produce rice of a subtly different flavour or texture. I find that one particular type will complement a particular meal better than another. Some people like rice which can be described as watery but personally I prefer a firmer variety of rice. I also think that the best rice is rice which is harvested in the autumn.

Ideally rice should be eaten plain – in other words without covering it in sauces or frying it with other ingredients. That way you can really appreciate the subtle flavour of the grain itself, and once you've learnt to recognise it you'll be appalled at the sight of people pouring gallons of soy sauce onto their rice.

In our house we use probably at least twice as much rice as other traditional households – mainly because we have so many visitors. Most people these days have electric rice cookers, and many of them use the cooker to cook rice overnight so it's ready for the next morning, but I don't advocate this myself. I think that rice needs to be treated with respect and should be freshly prepared for each meal.

In fact, one of the main reasons I get up so early is to prepare rice, which we then have for breakfast, and to make lunchboxes for the family. My son loves onigiri (rice balls) in his lunchbox because, like sandwiches, they are easy to pick up and eat, and with a variety of fillings they are also very tasty. In fact nearly all traditional lunch boxes (called bento) will include rice, and, even though it's eaten cold, it's still delicious. For added flavour we sometimes sprinkle sesame seeds on top or place a pink umeboshi (pickled plum) in the centre – which looks pretty as well as tasting good.

Preparation for Rice Cooking:

Traditionally, Japanese rice needs to be washed extensively before cooking. This has changed recently with the introduction of 'musenmai' – rice that has already been washed. However, it is still difficult to find this pre-washed rice outside Japan, so I would like to explain how to wash Japanese rice.

My mother was really fussy about how the rice was washed and many women of her generation have tried and tested methods of cleaning the rice. I think the best way is to put the rice into a bowl of water and, using your hands, swill it around and then drain into a sieve. You will see that the water is a very milky colour – the rice needs to be washed until the water turns clear. You need to scoop the rice up through the water and then lightly press it down with the heel of your hands. Repeat this action around 20 times, drain, add more water and repeat until the water clears. It creates quite a rhythmic sound as the rice swishes around in the water.

On average, I think it should take around 2–3 minutes to complete the washing. Once the water is clear, drain it and leave it for 30 minutes before cooking. During this time the rice should visibly plump up.

Most Japanese households these days have electric rice cookers, which are very convenient and easy to use. If you have a rice cooker then use it.

Cooking Rice in a Saucepan:

Take a heavy bottomed saucepan and put in the rice and the cold water. You should use slightly more water than rice and no salt. Bring to the boil – when you hear it boil, put on a tight fitting lid and turn the heat down low and cook for a further 15 minutes. Turn off the heat and leave for a further 10 minutes. Do not take the lid off at any time during the cooking. After it has rested, take off the lid and stir the rice. To do this, you need to cut through the rice with a wooden spoon and turn the rice from the bottom to the top. Don't try to break up the rice too much, the idea is to stop it being one solid mass but not separate the grains as with long grain rice.

If you cook your rice like this, it should be perfect – sticky but with a slight bite. If you have never had Japanese rice before, you will perhaps be surprised by the way it sticks together – do not worry as this is correct for this type of rice; it makes it easier to eat with chopsticks. If you find you have cooked too much you can always freeze anything left over or use it in a lunch box. Japanese rice is really tasty, even cold.

How Much Rice?

As I mentioned in the introduction, I eat a lot of rice but I suggest that you use around 450g of uncooked rice with 600–650ml water for around 4 people. As a rough rule of thumb, 150g of uncooked rice makes 300–350g cooked rice. Each household will be different, so you might need to adjust according to your own taste.

Beef on Rice
Gyudon

As you will have noticed in this section there are a number of recipes where something is served on top of a bowl of rice. It is such an easy and quick way to eat, especially at lunchtime. This recipe features a richly-flavoured beef and onion topping. The combination of beef and onions gives it a sweet but spicy taste. You can use almost any type of beef, as the wine tenderises it.

(Serves 4)
500g onions
1 cup/200ml white wine
½ cup/100ml water
500g thinly sliced beef
¾ cup/150ml soy sauce
¾ cup/150ml mirin
4 tablespoons caster sugar
600g hot cooked rice
pickled ginger (beni shoga) – to taste

1 Cut the onions in half lengthways and then slice into half moons 1cm wide.

2 In a medium size saucepan, bring the wine and water to the boil over a moderate heat. Add the beef and simmer for a few minutes, skimming the surface of the broth as it foams. Add the soy sauce, mirin and sugar and cover with a drop lid of aluminium foil (see cooking note) and simmer for a few more minutes.

3 Remove the lid, add the onions and again simmer until the onions are transparent and soft.

4 Put the hot cooked rice into 4 bowls. Ladle the beef and onions, together with some soup from the pan onto each rice bowl and garnish with a little pickled red ginger.

Cooking Note:
In this recipe we use a drop lid (called an otoshi buta) which is a wooden lid which drops inside a saucepan and sits directly on top of the food. We use this cooking technique frequently as it reduces the amount of liquid needed for cooking and concentrates the flavour. These days, even in Japan, many people use a circle of aluminium foil instead of a wooden lid – the important thing is that this 'lid' rests on top of the food, in the pan.

Three Types of Mixed Rice
Maze Gohan

Rice is a wonderful ingredient to work with. I like taking cooked rice and mixing it with a variety of different flavours. I have created these 'dressings' with deliberately light flavours so they work well with both hot or cold rice. They can be used either on top of the rice or mixed into the rice and served as rice balls. Also, they can be made in advance and are useful to serve with many different dishes. Each recipe is for 4–5 servings and the photos below show all three dressings.

Mixed Mushrooms Dressing:
120g fresh shiitake mushrooms
100g shimeji mushrooms
100g maitake mushrooms
3 tablespoons soy sauce
2 tablespoons mirin
10g dried fish flakes (optional)
2 tablespoons white sesame seeds

Ingredients Note:
If you cannot get these Japanese mushrooms then use a mixture of whatever fresh mushrooms you can obtain.

1 Remove the stems from all the mushrooms and wipe clean. Cut the shiitake mushrooms into 4 pieces. Divide the maitake and shimeji mushrooms into small bunches.
2 Put the soy sauce and mirin into a small pan and bring to the boil. Add all the mushrooms to the pan and cook on a moderate heat until the liquid has been absorbed. Add the dried fish flakes and toss all the ingredients together. Sprinkle the sesame seeds on top.

Salmon Dressing:
240g salmon
2 tablespoons sake
2 teaspoons mirin
1 teaspoon salt
a little light soy sauce

1 Place the salmon on a microwave resistant plate and sprinkle the sake on top. Cover with a lid and place in the microwave (600w) for 2½ minutes. Leave to cool.
2 Discard any bones or skin from the salmon and then roughly flake the flesh.
3 Put the cooked salmon in a pan with the mirin and salt and cook for a few minutes on a medium heat. Finally, season with the light soy sauce. If you are serving this as rice balls place a little salmon roe on top to add colour – and taste.

Spicy clam dressing:
150g cooked tinned asari clams or baby clams
15g piece of peeled ginger
1 tablespoon sake
1 tablespoon caster sugar
3 tablespoons soy sauce
2 tablespoons mirin

1 Drain the clams.
2 Cut the ginger into fine juliennes.
3 Put the clams and the sake into a small pan and cook over moderate heat for a few minutes. Add the sugar, soy sauce and mirin. Finally, add the ginger and cook until the liquid has been absorbed.

Japanese Style Green Risotto
Aona Zosui

This simple Japanese style risotto makes an excellent breakfast on cold mornings
or it can be served as a light meal during the rest of the day. A Japanese breakfast often
starts with rice and eggs and this recipe is very much in keeping with this tradition,
but the greens add a more contemporary slant to it. I use two or three different kinds
of green leaves – whatever I have in the fridge at the time.

(Serves 4)
4 eggs
25g Japanese parsley (seri – similar in flavour
   to flat leaf parsley)
100g shungiku (chrysanthemum leaves –
   rocket could be a suitable subsitute)
50g mitsuba (a little like coriander)
4 cups/800ml dashi or fish stock
1 tablespoon light soy sauce
½ teaspoon salt
150g cooked rice (preferably Japanese style rice)
soy sauce – to taste

1 Make Hot Spring Style Eggs. (See page 75 Tofu with
Hot Spring Egg).
2 Put the Japanese parsley, shungiku and mitsuba in a pan
of boiling water for about 30 seconds each, then drain and
soak in iced water. Squeeze the leaves lightly and chop into
1cm length pieces. (Follow this method if you are using other
green leaves – though if they are thicker than parsley they
might need to be cooked a little longer)
3 Put the dashi stock, light soy sauce and salt in a saucepan
and heat. Once it has come to the boil, add the
rice and turn down the heat so that it simmers gently.
Stir constantly and, when it thickens, turn off the heat.
Squeeze the greens again, add to the pan and mix in.
4 Divide between 4 bowls placing a hot spring egg on top
of each. Season with soy sauce to taste.

Fried Rice with Octopus

Tako Chahan

Simple stir fried dishes like this, or the stir fried noodles in the previous section, are very popular – especially with students who will create endless versions of this dish using whatever they have to hand. The secret is to make sure it is well seasoned and served piping hot.

(Serves 4)
160g cooked octopus legs
20g dried shiitake mushrooms
60g green pepper
100g spring onions
8g garlic (1 clove)
2 tablespoons sunflower or vegetable oil
600g hot cooked rice (preferably Japanese rice)
1 tablespoon oyster sauce
½ tablespoon soy sauce
salt and pepper – to taste
a pinch of granulated chicken stock
1 tablespoon sesame oil

1 Slice the octopus thinly. Soak the dried shiitake mushrooms in water until re-hydrated. Squeeze lightly and then roughly chop the mushrooms, green pepper and spring onions. Finely mince the garlic.
2 Heat the sunflower oil in a frying pan on a moderate heat. Add the chopped garlic and fry for a minute or so, until the garlic aroma is released, then add the sliced octopus and heat through. Remove to stop it getting too tough but keep it ready to add later.
3 Add the spring onions, green peppers and shiitake mushrooms and fry again.
4 Stir in the hot rice, mixing well and season with oyster sauce, soy sauce, salt, pepper and granulated stock.
5 Finally mix in the octopus, season with the sesame oil and serve immediately.

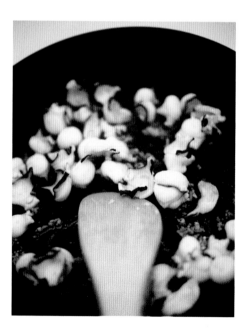

Ingredients Note:
If you can't get octopus ready cooked then you'll have to prepare it yourself. Have your fishmonger cut off the body then take the legs (which you are going to eat) and sprinkle with a little salt – too much will make it chewy. Rub the legs to get rid of any stickiness and then wash thoroughly under cold running water. Boil for 2–3 minutes, drain, leave to cool and pat dry.

Garlic Fried Rice
Ninniku Chahan

This fried rice smells amazing and is so quick to do. I often serve this up as an accompaniment to steak. If you have the time, I like to shape individual portions with a small mould, using something like a ramekin dish, and then turn it out onto the plate. It is easy to do but looks so impressive!

(Serves 4)
8–16g garlic (1–2 cloves)
10 shiso leaves or a mix of fresh basil
    and mint leaves
2 tablespoons sunflower or vegetable oil
450g cooked rice – Japanese if possible
1 teaspoon granulated chicken stock
soy sauce
dried fish flakes (if available)
coarsely ground pepper

1 Finely chop the garlic and then cut the shiso leaves into 8mm square pieces.

2 Heat the oil in a wok and fry the garlic, until you can smell it. Then add the rice and stock powder.

3 Add the soy sauce by pouring it onto the inside surface of the pan and mixing it in. Turn off the heat, add the shiso leaves and mix quickly, then serve either in the way I described above or on one large plate. Use the dried fish flakes and pepper as garnish.

Finely Chopped Tuna on Rice
Maguro no Tataki Don

I use tuna so frequently that I find it handy to keep some in the freezer, available for whenever I need it. For this recipe I like to chop the tuna in two different ways; half finely chopped and half roughly chopped. As you might have noticed with my recipes, I like to pay attention to how things are cut – I think this may be a rather Japanese tendency. Cutting ingredients in a variety of ways creates different textures as well as making a dish look different. Try it and see if you notice a difference.

(Serves 4)
100–200g sashimi-quality raw tuna
50g spring onions or shallots
20–25g myoga (optional)
10 shiso leaves or a mix of fresh basil and mint
15g freshly grated ginger
salmon roe – to taste
550g cooked rice – Japanese if possible
a little shredded daikon (mooli or Japanese
   white radish)
4 egg yolks – optional
soy sauce – to taste

Ingredients Note:
There are many different cuts of raw tuna for sashimi but for this recipe I like to use medium fatty tuna, chutoro. The most highly valued tuna is the really fatty tuna, or otoro, which just melts in the mouth.

1   Chop half of the tuna finely, and the rest roughly.
2   Chop the spring onion, myoga and shiso leaves roughly.
3   Then put the tuna, vegetables, grated ginger and salmon roe in a bowl and mix lightly.
4   Chop the white radish into thin matchsticks. Put some hot rice into four bowls and top with the white radish and then the tuna mix. I like to serve this with a raw egg yolk, so if you want to do this make sure the eggs are very fresh. Make a small well in the centre of the tuna mix and pop in the egg yolk. Add some soy sauce to taste.

Tofu

I am sure that many people outside Asia wonder what on earth to do with tofu – it seems to be such an alien taste and texture for westerners. However, if you try the following recipes I'm sure you will find that it is a wonderful and versatile ingredient.

In Japan we used to have specialist tofu makers who, like the bakers of Europe, would get up early every morning to prepare this essential food, so it was fresh for the day ahead.

Nowadays there are not many old style tofu makers left, and most people buy tofu from their local supermarket. Outside of Japan you can usually find it in your local health food shop or in the vegetarian section of many large supermarkets.

There are two types of tofu – soft (silken tofu or kinugoshi) and hard or firm (cotton tofu or momengoshi). The texture of tofu is part of its appeal, and, as the texture of one is quite different from the other, you may find you prefer a particular style. Personally I always use the soft or silken type. The only time I use firm tofu is for frying, because it holds its shape better.

Most Japanese like tofu, and eat it in many different ways. We have it hot in soups, we include it in stews in winter and eat it cold with various dressings in summer.

In fact I think tofu is such a healthy, cheap and versatile ingredient that I hope you will come to enjoy it and use it as frequently as I do.

Tofu with Basil and Gorgonzola Dressing

This is a rather Italian way to serve up tofu but I think the strong flavours of basil and gorgonzola work well with the mild flavour of the tofu. Despite a traditional aversion to cheese, modern Japanese are beginning to enjoy the many types available – even strong ones like gorgonzola!

For this recipe, I think it's better to break the tofu into pieces with your hands rather than to cut it with a knife, as this ensures that the dressing coats the tofu more effectively. Shop bought pesto sauce is usually too thick to use as a dressing for tofu, so this recipe thins it down with the addition of some stock.

(Serves 4)
300g firm/cotton tofu (1 pack)
2 tablespoons pesto sauce
1 tablespoon liquid chicken stock
1 medium tomato
ripe gorgonzola – to taste
fresh basil leaves – to garnish

1 Drain off the water from the tofu, wrap in kitchen paper and leave to drain.
2 Mix the pesto sauce with the chicken stock – adding more or less according to the liquidity of the pesto sauce. The final sauce should be quite runny.
3 Chop the tomato into small pieces and tear up the basil leaves.
4 Divide the tofu into four bowls and, using half the pesto mix, pour a little over each piece of tofu. Then crumble some gorgonzola over and sprinkle with the chopped tomato and basil leaves. Finally, pour the remaining pesto mix over the top.

Fried Tofu with Bean Sprouts and Pak Choy
Tofu to Moyashi no Chingensai Itame

I have a passion for bean sprouts and recommend that you take the time to top and tail each sprout. It really does make a difference. The key to success with this recipe is removing excess moisture from the tofu and then cooking it in hot sesame oil.

(Serves 4)
300g firm/cotton tofu (1 pack)
250g bean sprouts
100g pak choy
1 tablespoon sesame oil
1 tablespoon sunflower or vegetable oil
2 teaspoons granulated chicken stock
salt and pepper
coarsely ground white sesame seeds – to taste

1 Drain the tofu and then wrap in kitchen paper and place in a sieve for 30 minutes to remove excess water.

2 Discard the roots from the bean sprouts and wash, then drain well.

3 Cut the white stems of the pak choy lengthways into 3–4cm and chop the green leaves horizontally into 3–4cm pieces.

4 Heat the sesame oil in a frying pan. Break up the tofu by hand and fry for a few minutes. When it is really sizzling, remove from the pan and place it on a dish.

5 Add the sunflower oil to the frying pan and heat, add the pak choy and then the bean sprouts. Return the tofu to the pan, mix with the vegetables and season with the chicken stock powder and salt and pepper.

6 Put the cooked tofu and vegetables into an attractive serving dish and sprinkle with the sesame seeds.

Deep Fried Tofu with Japanese Dressing
Agedashi Dofu

This is a wonderful classic recipe, delicious all year round. The key is to get the tofu crispy and the correct flavour for the dressing.

(Serves 4)
600g soft/silken tofu (2 packs)
potato starch or cornflour for dusting
   the tofu pieces
oil – enough to deep fry the tofu
1 cup/200ml dashi stock or fish stock
2 tablespoons mirin
2 tablespoons soy sauce
a little caster sugar
a little salt
grated daikon (mooli or Japanese white radish)
grated ginger – to taste
shiso leaves, chopped into thin strips or a mix
   of fresh basil and mint leaves
myoga, chopped into 1–2mm pieces (optional)
spring onion or chives chopped into 1–2mm pieces

Ingredients Note:
Daikon is a very commonly used vegetable in Japanese cooking. This recipe does not use much but if you can find some it is a great 'extra' flavour and texture for this dish. It is often served in this way, raw and grated, as an accompaniment to grilled or fried dishes.

1 Drain the tofu and then wrap it in kitchen paper and place in a sieve for 30 minutes to remove excess moisture.
2 Cut the tofu into four pieces, dry again with kitchen paper, then coat with the potato starch.
3 Heat the oil to a suitable temperature for deep frying (around 170C). Carefully put the tofu pieces in to fry, and when they turn golden remove and drain on kitchen paper to remove excess oil.
4 In a small pan heat up the dashi stock, mirin, soy sauce, sugar and salt. Bring to the boil, ensuring that the sugar has dissolved.
5 Divide the tofu between four bowls. Pour a little of the hot sauce into each bowl and garnish with the grated daikon, a dab of grated ginger, shiso, myoga and spring onion to taste.

Tofu with Hot Spring Egg 'Onsen Tamago'
Onsen Tamago Nose Dofu

I think the best way to enjoy tofu is to eat it in the simplest possible way so you get to really appreciate the subtle and delicate taste of the tofu itself. Then you can add depth with tasty condiments and toppings. This particular recipe is simplicity itself and shows just how versatile and delicious tofu can be.

(Serves 4)
600g soft/silken tofu (2 packs)
4 hot spring eggs (see following recipe)
5g dried fish flakes
¼ cup/50ml soy sauce
2 tablespoons mirin
1 tablespoon sake
chopped spring onions or chives – to taste
grated fresh ginger – to taste

How to make 'Hot Spring Eggs' (onsen tamago)
  Put the eggs into a wide neck flask (or any other container that will hold heat) – make sure they are at room temperature, not chilled. Add boiling water to cover them and leave for 10 minutes. The yolk should still be runny with the white just cooked. It couldn't be easier.
  There are many hot springs in Japan – the result of the volcanic make up of the country – and eggs are often cooked in the boiling waters of the hot spring. The eggs take on a very strong sulphuric flavour that is popular with the Japanese but not always with visitors from overseas.

1 Drain the tofu and wrap in kitchen paper to remove excess water.
2 Make the dressing by combining the dried fish flakes, soy sauce, mirin and sake in a heat-resistant bowl and cooking it in the microwave for 2 minutes (600w). Leave to cool and then strain. If you cannot obtain the fish flakes then use a little concentrated fish stock to give a slight fish flavour to the dressing.
3 Cut the tofu into 4 pieces and place one piece in each bowl. Scoop out a hollow in each one and put a 'hot spring egg' in each hollow.
4 Arrange the scooped tofu around the edge. Scatter some spring onions on top and dab on a little grated ginger.
5 Pour the dressing over the tofu and serve.

Tofu Steak

I think that tofu novices are amazed that tofu can be as good as this. Tofu in this recipe is cooked in a similar way to steak – seasoned with salt, pepper and garlic and then sizzled. It should be cooked so that the outside is crispy and the inside hot. Serve it with lots of different vegetables and eat with soy sauce and Japanese wasabi (horseradish).

(Serves 4)
600g tofu (either type of tofu is fine but
   I prefer the soft/silken type – 2 packs)
90g red pepper
90g yellow pepper
80g courgette
200g fresh green asparagus
100g maitake mushrooms or other
   fresh mushrooms
300g tomatoes
16g garlic (2 cloves)
a little crushed garlic
a little pepper and salt
a little plain flour
4 tablespoons olive oil
soy sauce and wasabi – to taste

1 Drain the tofu, wrap in kitchen paper and place in a sieve for 30 minutes to remove any excess water.
2 Cut the peppers lengthways and remove the seeds. Slice into 3 lengthways. Cut the courgette into 2–3cm round slices. Cut off woody parts of the asparagus. Roughly tear up the maitake mushrooms. Cut the tomatoes in half. Peel the garlic cloves.
3 Heat half the olive oil in a frying pan and add the garlic. When you can smell the garlic, add the vegetables and let them sizzle for 5 minutes. Remove and place on a warm plate.
4 Cut the tofu into four pieces and season them with salt, pepper and minced garlic. Dust lightly with flour. Add the remaining olive oil to the frying pan and heat to a fairly high temperature. Place the tofu in the oil, then when it turns crispy on one side turn it over, then repeat on all sides. Remove when each piece is crispy and golden.
5 Serve with the cooked vegetables and a mixture of soy sauce and wasabi.

Tofu and Minced Pork Kebabs
Tofu no Tsukune

These kebabs have a slight south east Asian flavour to them with the addition of coriander and Thai fish sauce. The addition of tofu helps make these kebabs a little lighter and healthier than kebabs made only with meat.

(Makes 8 Kebabs)
300g firm/cotton tofu (1 pack)
50g green beans
small bunch fresh mint leaves
small bunch fresh coriander leaves
200g minced pork
50g finely chopped onion

For the marinade:
2 teaspoons Thai fish sauce
1 teaspoon light soy sauce
1 teaspoon of the juice from some grated ginger
a little salt
2 tablespoons sunflower or vegetable oil
serve with sanchu, coriander, sweet chilli sauce
 and lemon juice – to taste

1 Wrap the tofu in kitchen paper and place in a sieve for 30 minutes to remove excess water.
2 Top and tail the green beans and boil them until they are just cooked. Drain and then soak in chilled water. When cooled, drain again and cut into 1cm long pieces.
3 Chop the mint and coriander leaves roughly and mix.
4 Put the minced pork and the ingredients for the marinade into a bowl and mix well by hand until it becomes sticky.
5 Break the tofu into small pieces by hand and add to the mince mixture along with the beans, coriander, mint and onion. Mix thoroughly again – I find it best to do this by hand.
6 Divide the mixture into 8 pieces and shape each one into a sausage shape. Heat the oil in a frying pan and fry the kebabs until they brown on the outside and are cooked right through.
7 If you want, put a skewer in each kebab and arrange on a plate (you can also serve these like hamburgers). Serve with some sanchu and coriander, sweet chilli sauce and lemon wedges.

Ingredients Note:
Sanchu is a type of lettuce leaf which resembles round lettuce and is not crunchy like cos or iceburg.

Tofu and Avocado Dressing

This beautiful pale green coloured sauce is a very useful addition to many meals.
I particularly like serving it with deep fried chicken pieces or with grilled prawns
or fish. The combination of avocado and tofu gives it a real richness and a melt
in the mouth texture that is quite special.

150g soft/silken tofu (½ pack)
200g ripe avocado
a little lemon juice
3 tablespoons cottage cheese
1½ teaspoons granulated chicken stock
2 tablespoons mayonnaise
salt and pepper

Ingredients Note:
It is quite important with this recipe to use
soft/silken (or kinugoshidofu) tofu. If you
use the firm type it will be much more
difficult to achieve the necessary texture.

1. Wrap the tofu in kitchen paper and place on a sieve
for 30 minutes to drain.
2. Peel the avocado, take out the seed and put the flesh in a
mixing bowl. Add a little lemon juice and mash. Cut or break
the tofu into bite size pieces, add to the avocado and mix
together with the cottage cheese. Mix well using a balloon whisk.
3. Finally add the granulated stock, mayonnaise and salt and
pepper and serve immediately.

Hot Tofu with Ponzu Soy Sauce

Tofu makes a very welcome addition to any casserole dish. The tofu takes on the flavour of the stock and becomes quite a feast – as with shabu shabu (see page 120). In this recipe the tofu is cooked in a tasty stock and then dipped into ponzu soy sauce and it's especially comforting in winter.

(Serves 4)
4 cups/800ml dashi stock or fish stock
2 sheets 10cm square kombu seaweed
600g soft/silken tofu (2 packs)
200g baby leeks or large spring onions
100g enoki mushrooms
chopped spring onions or chives – to garnish
shichimi togarashi (a mixture of red pepper
    and other spices)

Ponzu Soy Sauce:
½ cup/100ml yuzu or kabosu juice
    (see Ingredients Note)
½ cup/100ml mirin
¾ cup/150ml soy sauce
¼ cup/50ml light soy sauce
10cm square kombu seaweed
    (wipe off any excess saltiness)

Ingredients Note:
Yuzu and kabosu are Japanese citrus fruits;
yuzu is similar to a lime and kabosu to a lemon,
so if you cannot find them then use lemons
or limes.

1 Pour the dashi stock into a casserole dish and add the kombu
seaweed. Leave for 30 minutes.
2 Cut the tofu into 6 square pieces. Slice the leeks diagonally
into 2cm wide pieces. Chop off the bottom part of the enoki
mushrooms and discard.
3 Place the casserole dish onto a medium heat and bring it to
a boil. Turn down to a simmer and add the tofu. When it comes
back to the boil again, add the leeks and mushrooms. Cook on
a gentle heat until the leeks are tender. Serve with the ponzu soy
sauce, chopped spring onions and the shichimi togarashi.

Ponzu Soy Sauce:
1 Squeeze 100ml of juice from the citrus fruits, making sure
to remove any pips.
2 Add the mirin to the citric juice and microwave uncovered
for 3 minutes (600w) and leave to cool
3 Add the two types of soy sauce and mix well.
4 Put into a sterilised bottle with the piece of kombu seaweed.
It will keep in the fridge for up to a month.

Seafood

I was fortunate to grow up in a village next to the sea where there was an endless supply of delicious fresh fish. My mother, like the other women of the village, knew the local fishmonger and would buy fish according to the season. These days we go to the supermarket and can find almost any type of fish all through the year, but if you can buy seasonally you will find a great improvement in flavour.

Traditionally, a basic meal in a Japanese home would consist of misoshiru (miso soup), rice, pickles and fish. Often the fish would be grilled whole and served up individually on rectangular plates. We like to see the shape of the fish and we're not afraid to eat parts of the fish, like the eyes, that many in the west find unacceptable.

We serve up fish and seafood in many ways. In the days before refrigeration we had to devise ways of preserving fish – using miso, salt, vinegar or even drying it. Like the Portuguese bacalao, even though these techniques are no longer strictly necessary for preservation, we still use them, as we enjoy the taste and the romance of them.

Nevertheless, to a Japanese person, the best way to enjoy fish and seafood is to eat it raw, as sashimi or in sushi – though it needs to be really fresh to be eaten this way. If you visit Japan it is worth visiting the fresh fish section in supermarkets and department stores or, even better, the famous Tokyo fish market, 'Tsukiji' – the biggest in the world – where you can see a bewildering variety of fish, including many species which are unavailable outside Asia.

My family consumes vast quantities of fish – I think we probably are the number one consumers of fish in the area in which I live!

Salmon Burgers

I think that the Japanese are very creative in taking dishes from around the world and adapting and recreating them to our taste. Most Japanese love fish and many also love burgers – which gave me the inspiration for the following recipe. The texture of this burger is quite different from beef burgers, which I think can be too dry. These salmon burgers are really juicy and can be served with different sauces for different tastes.

(Serves 4)
300g fresh salmon
100g onion
14g butter
150g potato, peeled
100g minced or coarsely chopped pork
a little beaten egg
salt and pepper – to taste
sunflower or vegetable oil for frying

Soy Dressing:
3 tablespoons soy sauce
1 tablespoon lemon juice
1 teaspoon chilli paste or to-ban-jan
caster sugar – to taste
a small handful of freshly chopped coriander
   leaves – to garnish

Other Suggested Toppings:
mayonnaise with coarsely ground pepper –
   to taste
pesto sauce

1 Remove any bones or skin from the salmon. Chop finely until it is almost minced.

2 Chop the onion into 7–8 mm pieces and cook lightly in the butter, taking care to retain the onion's crisp texture. Leave to cool.

3 Rinse the potato and cut in half widthways. Cover and heat in a microwave (600w) for 2–3 minutes until cooked (some potatoes may take longer). Mash and leave to cool (do not add any butter or milk).

4 In a large bowl mix the chopped salmon and minced pork. Add the cooked onion, mashed potato and beaten egg, then season with salt and pepper.

5 Shape the mixture into 12 small burgers. Heat the oil in a frying pan. Place the burgers in the pan and cook evenly on both sides.

6 Serve on plates with one of the toppings according to taste.

White Fish and Mozzarella Carpaccio Salad

This salad is a lovely combination of subtle flavours and colours. Raw fish work surprisingly well in this way. In the original recipe I used raw sea bream which I had previously wrapped in seaweed to give it more flavour. If you have the time to try this I have included the recipe below. Wrapping in kombu is a common method of preserving fish and it allows the fish to be eaten raw for up to two days, as well as adding extra taste and interest. You can use any sashimi-quality white fish for this recipe.

(Serves 4)
200g red onion
300g seaweed-marinated sea bream sashimi
(see below) or any other white fish sashimi
50g mozzarella cheese
salt and coarsely ground black pepper
olive oil
lemon juice

1 Cut the red onion into wafer thin half moon slices, and immerse in cold water for 5–10 minutes to remove any excess bitterness. Drain, pat dry and place on a serving plate.
2 Slice sea bream at an angle as thinly as you can manage (use your sharpest knife for this) and arrange the slices on top of the onions.
3 Place the mozzarella cheese on top, in the middle. Season with salt and pepper and drizzle over a little olive oil and fresh lemon juice.

(Serves 4)
300g sashimi-quality piece of sea bream
(you can also use other white fish sashimi)
1 teaspoon salt
2 pieces kombu seaweed of a suitable size
to cover the fish

Seaweed-Marinated Sea Bream

1 Season both sides of the sea bream with the teaspoon of salt and leave for 1 hour.
2 Wash away the salt and wipe off the excess water.
3 Wash the kombu seaweed lightly and wipe off the excess water. Put the sea bream between two pieces of kombu seaweed and wrap in cling film. Leave it in the fridge for half a day. The flavour of the seaweed works really well with the sea bream.

Sauté Squid Japanese Style
Ika no Sauté

Squid and octopus are both very popular in Japan and this is a very simple but tasty way to prepare squid.

(Serves 4)
¼ cup/50ml soy sauce
¼ cup/50ml mirin
1 teaspoon caster sugar
700g fresh squid
chilli powder or shichimi togarashi – to taste
   (see Ingredients Note)

Ingredients Note:
Shichimi togarashi is a frequently used spice mix containing seven different spices like sansho (a Japanese pepper) and black sesame. However, the over-riding flavour is of chilli.

1 Put the soy sauce, mirin and sugar into a small pan and bring to the boil on a moderate heat. Then turn the heat down and simmer for 2–3 minutes. When you can see the sauce thickening a little bit, remove from the heat and let it cool.
2 Remove the squid tentacles and discard the guts. Wash the bodies and tentacles.
3 Marinate in the cooled sauce for about 30 minutes.
4 If you have a griddle or fish rack then use it. If not use a regular grill or a frying pan on a medium heat. Make sure that you don't over cook the squid and its tentacles, just cook until it changes colour.
5 Once it's cooked, cut into thin rings and serve immediately with the chilli powder or the shichimi togarashi.

Mackerel Grilled with Salt
Saba no Shio Yaki

There are several common ways of cooking fish in Japan; one way is with a teriyaki sauce, and another is with salt or 'shio yaki'. Despite being told to cut down on our salt intake, we really like this style of cooking and I think it is a good way to cook almost any type of fish. I often serve this with a wedge of 'sudachi', which is one of the citrus fruits available in Japan and hard to find elsewhere. If you want to add a citrus flavour but can't find sudachi, use lime or lemon. Please note that although this recipe involves cooking the fish in an oven, it is also perfectly acceptable to grill the seasoned fish instead.

(Serves 4)
600g fresh mackerel fillets
salt and pepper
250g bean sprouts
80g mange tout
2 tablespoons sunflower or vegetable oil
8g thinly sliced garlic (1 clove)
2 teaspoons soy sauce

1 Season the mackerel fillets with salt and pepper and place skin side up on a baking tray lined with greaseproof paper.

2 Put in a pre-heated oven (230c) and cook for 15 to 20 minutes.

3 Prepare the bean sprouts by topping and tailing them (it makes a difference to the final taste). String the mange tout and blanch in a small pan of boiling water. Drain and then plunge in cold water for 5 minutes. Drain again, dry and then slice finely on the diagonal.

4 When the fish is almost ready to serve, cook the garlic in the oil in a frying pan or wok. When its aroma is released, add the bean sprouts and mange tout and cook quickly. Season with a little soy sauce and pepper.

5 Tip the piping hot vegetables onto a serving plate and place the mackerel fillets on top.

Tuna Carpaccio

It is amazing how many recipes can be created using raw fish. It's too easy to think only of eating it in the classical way with just wasabi and soy sauce. I hope that this recipe will help you see alternative ways of eating raw fish.

(Serves 4)
10 shiso leaves or a mix of fresh basil
   and mint leaves
180g Japanese white daikon
   (mooli or Japanese white radish)
100–120g sashimi-quality raw tuna
50ml mayonnaise
1 tablespoon milk
1 teaspoon light soy sauce
½ teaspoon mustard
a little white pepper

Ingredients Note:
Daikon is a large, white radish which is often served raw, either shredded or grated. It is sometimes known as mooli and can often be found in Chinese supermarkets or in other ethnic supermarkets. If you cannot find it a little shredded raw cabbage or even shredded iceburg or cos lettuce would work.

1 Shred the shiso and daikon (mooli or Japanese white radish) and freshen by soaking in water for a minute, then gently squeeze to remove any excess water and put in a serving bowl.

2 Slice the tuna finely at an angle and arrange the slices on top of the salad.

3 Mix the mayonnaise, milk, light soy sauce, mustard and white pepper to make a dressing and drizzle it on top of the salad.

Octopus Tomato and Parsley Salad

The sweetness of the tomatoes and the bitterness of the parsley bring out the flavour of the octopus in this recipe. Octopus can be a little tough so it is as well to make sure that it is cut into fairly small pieces. You could also use squid as a substitute in the same way. This goes very well with white wine.

(Serves 4)
200g cooked octopus legs
450–600g tomatoes
25g parsley
3 tablespoons olive oil
2 tablespoons white wine vinegar
1 tablespoon balsamic vinegar
1 teaspoon light soy sauce
salt and pepper

Ingredients Note:
I like to mix these two different vinegars –
wine vinegar is a little too sharp on its own
and balsamic is too sweet – so mixing them
gives a well-balanced flavour to the dressing.
(see page 64 for how to cook octopus)

1 Cut the octopus into 1–2 cm square pieces. Cut the tomatoes into pieces the same size as the octopus.
2 Discard the parsley stems and then roughly chop the leaves.
3 Mix the olive oil, white wine vinegar, balsamic vinegar, soy sauce and salt and pepper in a bowl. Add the octopus and the tomatoes.
4 Mix thoroughly and put onto a serving plate or bowl. Sprinkle the chopped parsley on top.

Salmon Teriyaki

This sauce has already proved to be popular around the world and you can buy the ready made versions from most large supermarkets. However, it is such a simple sauce to make that it is worth making it yourself.

(Serves 4)
320g fresh salmon
200g baby leeks
200g eringi mushrooms
200g maitake mushrooms
4½ tablespoons sunflower or vegetable oil
sudachi or lemon or lime – to taste
mustard – to taste

For the Teriyaki Sauce:
¼ cup/50ml soy sauce
1 tablespoon mirin
1 teaspoon caster sugar

Ingredients Note:
You may not be able to find the eringi or maitake mushrooms so substitute other types of mushrooms that are available – most should work well with this salmon.

1 Marinate the salmon in the teriyaki sauce for an hour.
2 Cut the baby leeks into 4cm long pieces. Slice the eringi mushrooms into 2–3 lengthways pieces. Cut off the stalk of the maitake mushrooms.
3 Line a baking tray with greaseproof paper and place the salmon on it. Place in a pre-heated oven (230c) for 15 minutes, brushing the salmon with the sauce two or three times during cooking.
4 Put ½ a tablespoon of the oil in a frying pan and add the baby leeks. Cook them on quite a high heat and keep pressing them well into the pan to ensure that they cook. As they cook, they will become softer in texture – take them out when they are cooked to your taste.
5 Add the remaining oil and fry the mushrooms. When they are ready, place them and the leeks and the salmon on a plate and serve up with some sudachi and mustard.

Mackerel 'Tatsuta Age' Style
Saba no Tatsuta Age

Tatsuta age style of cooking is suitable for chicken as well as for fish. It is very simple and tastes good even when cold, and makes a useful addition to lunch boxes.
Fish or meat is first marinated in sake, mirin and soy sauce and then dipped into potato starch and quickly fried. It should be nice and crispy on the outside but still very moist on the inside.

(Serves 4)
430g fresh mackerel fillets
2 tablespoons sake
2 tablespoons soy sauce
½ tablespoon grated fresh ginger
1 tablespoon mirin
potato starch or cornflour for coating the mackerel
oil for deep frying
kinome (a Japanese herb) – if available or thinly
    sliced spring onion
sudachi or lemon or lime

1 Check the fillets for bones and then cut them into bite size pieces. Marinate them in the mix of sake, soy sauce, mirin and grated ginger for 10 minutes.
2 When you are ready to deep fry the fish (which should be at room temperature), take them out of the marinade and dip them into plenty of potato starch. Fry the fish immediately to ensure that it goes crispy on the outside. The oil should be around 170C and the fish should turn golden when cooked.
3 Serve immediately with wedges of sudachi, lemon or lime and the kinome leaves on top, if available.

Prawn and Squid Tempura
Gochiso Kakiage

This mixture of prawns, squid and leeks is best eaten piping hot. The main thing you should be aiming for is to make it really crispy. To do this you need to make the ingredients really cold before you deep fry them – including, surprisingly enough, chilling the flour mix. As you will see from the photo we use this recipe to make four crunchy tempura disks or 'rounds' which are served on top of a bowl of steaming hot rice. You can then either pour some of the tentsuyu sauce on top or have the sauce in a separate small bowl for each person to dip into. Alternatively, as with all types of tempura, you can dip into small dishes of salt and pepper or even chilli powder instead.

(Serves 4)
150g small prawns
100g fresh squid (without its tentacles)
200g baby leeks or spring onions
50g mitsuba (a Japanese herb like coriander)
½ tablespoon baking powder
1 cup/100g plain flour
½ beaten egg
a little cold water
oil for deep frying
2 tablespoons grated daikon
    (mooli or Japanese white radish)
2 teaspoons grated fresh ginger

For the Tentsuyu Tempura Dipping Sauce:
½ cup/100ml soy sauce
2 tablespoons sugar
¼ cup/50ml mirin
1 cup/200ml water
15g dried fish flakes
dashi stock – to dilute

Ingredients Note:
Tentsuyu is made from a basic sauce called mentsuyu diluted with dashi stock to reduce sweetness (so it is suitable for tempura).
To make the basic sauce, mentsuyu, take the above ingredients, except the dashi, mix in a bowl and microwave uncovered for 3 minutes (600w). Leave it to cool then strain it and it is ready for use.

1 Remove prawn shell, tail and gut, and chop into 3–4 pieces. Take off the thin membrane from the squid, score the surface with a knife then cut it into pieces of around 3cm.

2 Chop the leeks or onions into 1cm disks and tear the mitsuba leaves into pieces of about 2cm.

3 Put the baking powder and flour into a plastic bag and shake. Put the prawns, squid, baby leeks and mitsuba into the fridge for about half an hour to make sure they are really cold.

4 Once suitably chilled, mix the prawns, squid, leeks and mitsuba with 2 tablespoons of the flour mix and form into a ball. Put the remaining flour mix in a bowl, add ⅔ of a cup of liquid made up of half a beaten egg and cold water. Mix lightly.

5 Divide the prawn, squid and leeks mixture into four, and shape them roughly into flat 'rounds'.

6 Heat the oil to 170c. You can use a wok or a small saucepan but you need to have enough oil to deep fry one of the 'rounds' at a time.

7 Take a small plate and grease it with a little sunflower oil, then place one of the 'rounds' on top and pour over a quarter of the batter. Mix the batter in lightly and then slide the 'round' into the oil.

8 Cook until the colour changes, turning it half way through the cooking.

9 Repeat with the remaining three 'rounds'.

10 Serve on hot rice with the tentsuyu sauce, some grated daikon and grated ginger.

Chicken & Egg

I hope you will use the best chicken and eggs you can find for the recipes in this section as there is such an enormous difference between just average and really good quality. Also, I think that the skin and thighs are the tastiest parts of the chicken, so in my recipes I encourage you to use them.

Most traditional restaurants in Japan specialise in a specific type of cooking. One of the most popular types is yakitori – chicken kebabs. These restaurants, often tiny places, serve up almost every part of a chicken on a skewer. You can order skewers of just chicken skin, chicken thighs or chicken livers – a huge variety is possible. These skewers are usually cooked over charcoal and served up with ice-cold mugs of beer – delicious.

In Japan we are quite happy to eat eggs raw. For breakfast it's quite common to crack an egg onto steaming hot rice and then we eat it with just a drizzle of soy sauce – the heat of the rice cooks the egg. When you eat sukiyaki (beef hot pot) you dip the hot beef slices into raw egg before eating it. However, if you are going to eat eggs raw just remember to make sure that they are absolutely fresh and of the highest quality.

Leaf Wrapped Fried Chicken

Deep fried chicken pieces are very popular in Japan. They are used in lunch boxes, in bars as accompaniments to drinks as well as for general family meals. This dish takes deep fried chicken (tori no karaage) and serves it with fresh herbs and salad leaves. This allows everyone to make their own style of fried chicken roll – ready to dip into chilli sauce.

(Serves 2–3)
250g boneless chicken thighs with skin
3 tablespoons potato starch or cornflour
2 tablespoons plain flour
sunflower or vegetable oil for deep-frying

For the marinade:
1 tablespoon soy sauce
½ tablespoon shokoshu (Chinese sake)
½ teaspoon crushed garlic
salt

some salad leaves to wrap the chicken
fresh chives, mint, coriander – to taste
sweet chilli sauce (for dipping)

1 First make up the marinade. Pierce the chicken skin in several places before cutting each piece into 6 to 7 smaller pieces. Place them in the marinade and make sure that they are all well coated and leave them to marinate for around 30 minutes.

2 Lightly mix the potato starch and flour and then dust the marinated chicken pieces generously.

3 Heat the oil for frying (170c). When the oil is hot enough, deep-fry the chicken pieces for 4–5 minutes until crisp, golden and cooked through. To maintain the oil temperature, do not add too many chicken pieces at once (halve one chicken piece to check if it is cooked inside). Drain the cooked chicken on kitchen paper.

4 Serve the deep fried chicken with a selection of washed herbs and salad leaves. Wrap pieces of chicken in the leaves accompanied by herbs of your choice. Using your fingers to eat, dip in chilli sauce and enjoy!

Chicken Sauté Kari Kari Style

Crispy chicken is great with a mountain of chives on top. Use so many chives that you can hardly see the chicken underneath. This recipe also works well with duck or with chicken breast, if you prefer.

(Serves 4)
250g boneless chicken thighs with skin
salt and pepper
½ tablespoon sunflower or vegetable oil
75g chives
ponzu soy sauce – to taste (see page 80)
mustard – to taste

1 Prick the skin of the chicken with a fork then dry with kitchen paper. Season with salt and pepper.
2 Heat the oil in a frying pan and fry the chicken skin side down. When it turns golden brown turn it over and continue to cook, covering the chicken with a drop lid or circle of foil to keep it moist – see the Beef on Rice recipe for more information.
3 Chop the chives finely (2–3mm).
4 Cut the cooked chicken into bite size pieces, sprinkle with plenty of chives, pour over a little ponzu soy sauce and serve with a little mustard on the side.

Rice Topped with Raw Egg
Tamago Gake Gohan

This is such an easy meal – the original Japanese fast food! Although it's simple it's very tasty and one of my favourite ways to eat egg. It is also a very traditional dish for breakfast. This recipe uses quite a few typically Japanese toppings, so if you can't find them then try substituting them with what you can find locally.

(Serves 4)
600g hot cooked rice
4 fresh eggs
a little soy sauce

Suggested Traditional Toppings:
seaweed paste (iwa nori)
dried fish flakes
dried baby anchovies (chirimen zansho)
Japanese pickles
asari clams boiled down in soy (see the
  Maze Gohan recipe on page 60)

Ingredients Note:
Instead of the traditional toppings you can use ingredients you already have to hand like cooked spinach, salmon or tinned tuna. You can even have it with just the egg and soy sauce.

1 Fill a rice bowl with freshly cooked rice, crack an egg on top, then add your preferred toppings. Add the soy sauce and mix well.

Steamed Chicken Salad with Sesame Sauce
Mushi Dori no Gomadare Salad

Sesame sauce using the juices from cooked chicken is so easy to prepare. This style of dressing with sesame, gomadare, is very common in Japanese cooking and is used for both meat and vegetables. This particular chicken dish makes a lovely appetiser, but it also goes very well with cold noodles.

(Serves 4)
100g spring onion
200g cucumber (preferably small cucumbers)
250g boneless chicken thighs with skin
salt and pepper
1 tablespoon sake
1 teaspoon sesame oil
a small piece of crushed ginger

For the Sesame Sauce:
¼ cup/50ml liquid made up from the juices
  of the cooked chicken (and water if necessary)
4 tablespoons sesame paste
2 tablespoons soy sauce
2 tablespoons caster sugar
½ tablespoon rice vinegar
2 teaspoons chilli paste or to-ban-jan
2 tablespoons roughly ground sesame seeds
2 tablespoons finely shredded spring onions
2 teaspoons finely chopped ginger
2 teaspoons finely chopped garlic

Ingredients Note:
Gomadare – meaning 'dressed with sesame sauce' can be made either with ready made sesame paste or, more traditionally, by grinding toasted sesame seeds to a rough paste in a suribachi (pestle and mortar). Tahini, a Greek style sesame paste is a reasonable and easily available substitute, but as it is not made from toasted sesame there is a slight difference in flavour. Unsweetened peanut butter is another possible substitute.

1 Finely chop the spring onion diagonally, keeping back the green part for use during cooking the chicken. Soak in cold water for a few minutes to remove the bitterness of the onion, then drain and put aside to use later.

2 On a chopping board, sprinkle the cucumber with a few pinches of salt, rubbing it into the flesh, then rinse. This lessens the aroma of the cucumber and gives it a good green colour. Hit the cucumber with a pestle (if you don't have a pestle, use a bottle) and break it apart with your hands, to make uneven pieces.

3 Pierce the chicken pieces with a skewer and place in a heat-resistant bowl. Add the salt, pepper and oil and then place the green part of the spring onion and the crushed ginger on top. Cover and put in the microwave for 4 minutes (600w) or until cooked. Leave to cool. Keep the juice from the chicken to use in the sesame sauce.

4 Shred the chicken with your hands and place in a serving dish. Mix in the cucumber and put the chopped spring onion on top.

5 Mix all the ingredients for the sesame sauce in a small bowl and pour over the chicken and cucumber.

Chicken and French Beans with Basil Rice
Tori Adobo fu

I use a lot of green beans in my recipes as I love their taste, colour and crunch. In this recipe I use the slightly larger French beans but any green bean will be good. This meal goes well with boiled rice, but if served with basil rice it becomes even more of a feast.

(Serves 4)
500g boneless chicken thighs with skin
pepper
32g garlic (4 cloves)
360g French beans
½ tablespoon sunflower oil or vegetable oil
½ cup/100ml of rice vinegar
¼ cup/50ml sake
1½ cups/300ml water
½ cup/100ml soy sauce
1 bay leaf
1 teaspoon dried coriander
4 hard-boiled eggs (shelled)

1 Cut the chicken into 6 pieces. Season lightly with pepper. Peel the garlic cloves.
2 Remove the string from the French beans, top and tail and then lightly boil or steam. Drain while the beans are still very firm. Cut each bean into 3.
3 Heat the oil in a frying pan or wok on a moderate heat. Add the garlic, and when its aroma is released place the chicken, skin side down, into the pan. When the skin turns golden brown turn and brown the other side.
4 Add the rice vinegar, sake, water, soy sauce, bay leaf and coriander to the pan and simmer at low to moderate heat.
5 When the liquid has reduced by half, add the boiled eggs and the French beans. Simmer for 5 minutes and then serve.

For the Basil Rice:
(Serves 4)
2 handfuls fresh basil
2 tablespoons sunflower or vegetable oil
2 tablespoons finely chopped garlic
450g hot cooked rice – preferably Japanese rice
1 teaspoon granulated chicken stock
salt and pepper – to taste

1 Roughly chop the basil.
2 Heat the oil in a frying pan on a moderate heat. Add the garlic and fry gently. When you can smell the garlic, add the cooked rice and fry until heated through. Season with the granulated stock, salt and pepper. Turn off the heat and mix in the basil. Serve immediately.

Chicken with Red and Green Peppers

Tori to Piman no Itame ni

This is a really quick and delicious meal. The red and green peppers add a lovely colour but make sure not to overcook them – they should still have quite a bite to them. I like to serve this up with some Japanese white rice.

(Serves 4)
500g boneless chicken thighs with skin
100g finely chopped onion
1 tablespoon finely chopped garlic
¼ cup/50ml red wine
¼ cup/50ml soy sauce
fresh basil and rosemary
150g green pepper
90g red pepper
2 tablespoons olive or sunflower oil

1   Cut the chicken into 2cm size pieces. In a bowl, mix together the onion, garlic, red wine, soy sauce, basil and rosemary and use this as a marinade for the chicken while you prepare the peppers.

2   Cut the peppers in half and remove the seeds, then cut them lengthways into fairly thin strips.

3   Heat half of the olive oil (1 tablespoon) in a frying pan on a medium heat. Put in the chicken and brown on both sides, then cook on a medium heat until just cooked through. Remove from the pan.

4   Add the remaining oil and quickly fry the peppers. When they are just cooked, though still with a bite to them, return the chicken and any marinade sauce that remains, heat through. Serve hot.

Japanese Style Savoury Pancake
Okonomiyaki Hiroshima fu

Anyone who has been to Japan will probably have tasted 'okonomiyaki'. It is a cheap, popular family style of eating. There are many different recipes for 'okonomiyaki', with ingredients varying from region to region and household to household. Everyone has their favourite and mine is one that comes from the Hiroshima area. I love it so much that I will even travel to Hiroshima just to be able to eat their special 'okonomiyaki'!

'Okonomiyaki' is not a simple dish to make for the first time but it is worth trying and is almost a complete meal in itself. If you can get a table-top hot ring it is fun to cook this at the table with friends or family.

If this is the first time you have made these, it might be useful for you to imagine the final dish. Working from the bottom up, there is a pancake filled with cabbage, squid and pork, a layer of fried noodles and finally a couple of fried eggs on top. Quite a feast.

1 To make the batter: sift the flour and bicarbonate of soda into a bowl. Add the water and mirin and mix well.

2 Heat a little oil in a frying pan on a moderate heat. Pour in enough batter to make a thin 18cm size pancake.

3 Sprinkle a quarter of the chopped cabbage, bean sprouts, spring onions, dried fish flakes and chopped pork onto the batter. Season lightly with salt and pepper. Put the squid on top and cook – making sure that the pork and squid are properly cooked before going to the next stage.

4 Add 2 tablespoons of batter to the pancake then turn over and press lightly using a spatula.

5 In a separate frying pan heat a little more oil, then add the cooked noodles and fry lightly. Season with 1 tablespoon Worcester sauce, shape the noodles into a circle and transfer the previously cooked pancake on top.

6 Fry two eggs then put the pancake and noodles on top of the eggs and turn the whole thing over. Turn out onto a plate so that the eggs are on the top and the noodles underneath. Repeat this procedure using the rest of the ingredients.

7 To serve: mix the tonkatsu sauce, Worcester sauce and tomato ketchup and drizzle over the assembled pancake. If you have ao-nori seaweed, sprinkle it over and add the red ginger for garnish.

(Serves 4)
For the pancake batter:
100g plain flour
⅓ teaspoon bicarbonate of soda
1 cup/200ml water
1 teaspoon mirin

For the pancake filling:
200g shredded sweetheart or green cabbage
250g bean sprouts
180g thinly sliced squid (or to taste)
120g thinly sliced uncooked pork
finely chopped spring onions or chives – to taste
dried fish flakes – to taste
salt and pepper
a little sunflower or vegetable oil
600g cooked Chinese egg noodles
4 tablespoons Worcester sauce
8 eggs
4 tablespoons tonkatsu sauce – to taste
2 teaspoons Worcester sauce
1 tablespoon tomato ketchup
red pickled ginger (beni shoga) and ao-nori –
    to taste

Ingredients Note:
Ao-nori seaweed is a green dried seaweed often sprinkled on food to give extra flavour. Tonkatsu sauce is a rich dark sauce that can be obtained in Asian supermarkets.

Beef & Pork

Despite the fact that I love vegetables, I also really love meat. Steak is one of my three favourite dishes (the others being sashimi and tori no karaage). I just love steak – sirloin and fillet, thick cut, rare or thinly sliced – I could eat it any way. My husband is more particular and loves his beef thinly sliced and cooked in a traditional Japanese style such as 'shabu shabu' (beef and vegetables cooked in boiling water) or as 'sukiyaki' (a type of beef stew).

Even though we've only been eating beef in Japan for just over 150 years it's now become very popular, and good quality beef is inexpensive and easy to obtain. I often get some reasonably priced beef from the local supermarket and turn it into something interesting using a variety of seasonings – sometimes I cook it Japanese style, sometimes western style and sometimes Asian style. Beef can also be transformed by the type of vegetables you cook it with, and I love creating new recipes to change ordinary beef into something really special.

Pork is widely used in Japan and is often deep fried and served as tonkatsu, or fried on a skewer with onions and vegetables, as kushikatsu and sometimes sautéed.

Minced meat is also very popular and used in many ways. It is usually sold as a mix of beef and pork. Since the war hamburgers have become an increasingly normal part of our culture, but usually served with a Japanese twist – covered with a sauce or a fried egg – a little different from hamburgers American style.

Rare Beef Salad
Gyu Tataki Salad

Tataki style is a very common way of serving beef and some 'meatier' fish like tuna. It involves searing the meat or fish very quickly, then slicing it and eating it with tangy dipping sauces. This recipe is great for dinner parties as it can easily be prepared in advance. The dipping sauce, the mentsuyu, can also be made in advance and kept until needed.

(Serves 4)
500g joint of beef (preferably leg of beef)
salt and pepper – to season
1 teaspoon crushed garlic
sunflower or vegetable oil
6–7cm daikon (mooli or Japanese white radish)
small bunch of mitsuba (or coriander
   if unavailable)
5 shiso leaves or a mix of fresh mint and basil
1 bud of myoga – or 1–2 spring onions
mustard – to taste

For the Mentsuyu Sauce:
1 cup/200ml soy sauce
½ cup/100ml mirin
3 tablespoons caster sugar
1 cup/200ml water
20g dried fish flakes

Ingredients Note:
If you are unable to find these particular leaves for the salad, then use anything available, choosing textures that are crunchy and flavours that are sharp and tangy, such as rocket.
   If you cannot find the dried fish flakes, substitute the ½ cup/100ml of water for ½ cup/100ml of fish stock. It should not be a strong fishy flavour but just have a slight tang.

1 Make sure that the beef is at room temperature before you start. Season the joint with salt, pepper and garlic.

2 In a wok, heat the oil until very hot, then put the beef in and seal it on all sides. Remember that the beef will keep on cooking even after you have taken it out of the pan so adjust the cooking time accordingly.

3 Take the joint out of the pan and wrap it in foil.

4 Chop up the daikon into thin matchsticks. Cut the mitsuba into 2cm length pieces. Take the shiso leaves and first cut them in two down the centre and then chop them up finely.

5 If you have myoga slice it finely, or use finely chopped spring onions. Put the myoga in water for a couple of minutes then drain and dry well.

6 Now take all the chopped leaves and mix them. Take the beef, slice it finely and place the slices on top of the greens. Finish by dabbing some mustard on the beef slices.

7 To make the mentsuyu sauce: take all the ingredients and put them in a microwave proof bowl without a lid and cook for 3 minutes (600w). Leave to cool and strain. Leave in the fridge until required.

Steak Marinated in Two Types of Miso

Miso is not just for soups, it makes a tasty marinade for both fish and meat.
For this recipe I use two types of miso, the sweeter white miso and the saltier red
miso. I usually make my own miso each January or February, making enough for
the whole year. Although miso is excellent for health, it can be a little salty, so you
need to be careful not to overdo it.

(Serves 2)
50g white miso
50g red miso
½ tablespoon soy sauce
½ tablespoon sake
1 tablespoon mirin
200g fillet steak
sunflower or vegetable oil to pan fry the meat
wasabi – to taste

1   Mix together the two types of miso, soy sauce, sake and mirin.
Using a tablespoon of this sauce, marinate the fillet and wrap in
cling film and leave in the fridge for 2–3 hours. (You can keep the
remaining marinade sauce for up to four weeks in the fridge –
it doesn't change in flavour.)

2   About half an hour before you want to cook it take the meat
out of the fridge, so that it reaches room temperature.

3   Heat a little oil in a frying pan. Remove any excess marinade
from the fillet and then pan fry over a high heat.

4   When cooked (according to your own taste) serve garnished
with some wasabi. I often serve this with a green salad and some
rice that I have shaped in a ramekin and decorated with toasted
sesame seeds.

Beef and Vegetable Rolls
Gyuniku no Yasai Maki

I think it is a very Asian tendency to wrap things – the spring roll is a great example of this. This recipe uses beef instead of pastry as a wrap, and it works just as well with thinly sliced pork. The sauce is also so good that you can just marinate the beef in it and then cook and eat it as it is.

(Serves 4)
Sauce for the beef:
4 tablespoons soy sauce
1 tablespoon sake
2 tablespoons sesame oil
2 tablespoons caster sugar
2 tablespoons red wine
3 tablespoons ground sesame seeds
2 teaspoons finely crushed garlic
1 teaspoon grated fresh ginger
black pepper
chilli pepper or ichimi togarashi

200g fresh green asparagus
70–80g green beans
360g thinly sliced beef

1   Put all the ingredients for the sauce into a bowl and mix well, making sure the sugar dissolves. Leave it to mature for 2–3 hours.
2   Cut off the woody base and strip the side leaves from the asparagus. Top and tail the green beans. Cook the vegetables so they are still firm to the bite. Drain. Plunge into chilled water and drain again.
3   Pour around 50ml of the sauce on to the beef and mix it in thoroughly by hand.
4   Spread the beef slices out on a plate. Place a spear of asparagus and some green beans down the centre of each slice and then roll the beef around the vegetables, making a sausage shape. If there are not enough vegetables, then just roll some of the beef slices.
5   As the beef is so thin, these rolls cook very quickly. You can either grill them or pan fry them. You might find it easier if you put a skewer through them but they should stay together anyway.
6   Carefully cut the rolls into bite size pieces and place on a serving plate. Pour over the remaining sauce and serve with white rice.

Pot Roast Pork

I find this method of cooking a large joint of pork is the best – it remains more tender than if roasted in the oven. It is not something that I would do every day but it is great when you want to entertain and any left overs can be used in fried rice (chahan) or even in sandwiches.

(Serves 8)
2 kg joint of pork – preferably shoulder, without rind or bones
salt and coarsely ground black pepper – to taste
½ tablespoon sunflower or vegetable oil
3–4 bay leaves
string to tie the joint

Japanese Style Wasabi Sauce:
1 cup/200ml of juices made up from the cooked pork joint and chicken stock
2 tablespoons soy sauce
1 tablespoon of potato starch or cornflour mixed with 1 tablespoon of cold water
1 teaspoon wasabi

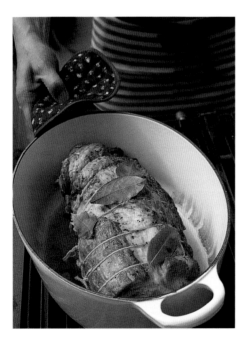

1   Season the pork joint with salt and pepper. Tie with string.
2   Put the oil in a large frying pan and bring it to a very high heat.
3   Place the joint in the pan and seal on all sides.
4   Remove from the heat and place in a very heavy casserole pan with a lid (I find that a Le Creuset is perfect for this). Put the bay leaves on top and cover loosely with some aluminium foil – this helps to keep the moisture in.
5   Cover with the lid and cook on a very low heat for about an hour, turning the meat once or twice during this period.
6   After checking that the meat is cooked (the juices should run clear when you put in a skewer) take the joint out of the pan and let it cool. When cooled, slice it as thinly as you can.
7   To make the Japanese style wasabi sauce, take the juices from the cooked joint, skim off the fat and then add some chicken stock to make up a cup of stock. Add the cornflour, and heat in a pan. When it starts to thicken, add the soy sauce. Finally add the wasabi. Place in a small jug and serve with the sliced roast pork.

Alternative dressing: Apple Mayonnaise Sauce
   Take 3 medium size apples and peel, core and then cut them into 8 segments. Put 1 cup of wine and ¼ cup of water into a pan and bring to a boil. Add the apple, cover with a drop lid or circle of foil, and simmer gently until most of the liquid has been absorbed and the apples are soft. Turn over once during cooking. Leave to cool.
   Then blend together the apple, 3–4 tablespoons mayonnaise, a tablespoon of finely chopped onion and salt and pepper to taste. If you are feeling lazy you can make this with shop bought apple sauce, but this method gives better results.

Japanese Pepper Steak with Ginger Mashed Potatoes

Japanese sansho pepper is different from black pepper in both aroma and flavour. Unfortunately, it is not very easy to find outside of Japan and China. The nearest seasoning that I can find is Szechwan pepper, so use that if you can't find sansho.

1 Make sure that the steaks are at room temperature and then season on both sides with a little salt and then lots of the sansho or Szechwan pepper.

2 Heat the oil in a frying pan and cook the steak to your liking.

3 Place the steak on a plate with a sprig of kinome on top. If you cannot find kinome then use a little cress. Serve with the ginger mashed potatoes.

Ginger Mashed Potatoes

1 Peel the potatoes and cut each one into 4. Soak in water for a few minutes then drain and dry.

2 Line a microwave resistant bowl with kitchen paper and add the potatoes. Lightly cover and place in the microwave (600w) for 5 minutes, or until cooked through.

3 Take the potatoes out while they are still hot and mash. Add the butter and milk and mix thoroughly. Add the cream and season with salt and pepper.

4 Put the soy sauce and mirin into a small pan and bring to the boil. Add the potato starch and simmer until thickened. Remove from the heat and mix in the grated ginger.

5 Place the mashed potato on a plate, make a hollow in the centre and pour in the ginger sauce to serve.

(Serves 4)
4 x 150g fillet steaks (3cm thick)
a little salt
plenty of coarsely ground sansho pepper
  or Szechwan pepper – to taste
sunflower or vegetable oil for pan frying
kinome leaf – if available

Ginger Mashed Potatoes
(Serves 4)
440g medium size potatoes
14g butter
½ cup/100ml milk
¼ cup/50ml double cream
salt and pepper
¼ cup/50ml soy sauce
¼ cup/50ml mirin
1 small tablespoon potato starch or cornflour
  mixed with 1 tablespoon water
1 tablespoon grated fresh ginger

Bite Size Steak Pieces with Japanese Vegetables
Koro Koro Steak Tataki fu

This steak dish makes a light and tasty meal and is good not only to eat but also to look at. This original recipe uses many Japanese vegetable ingredients but if you cannot find some of them then use what you have locally such as watercress, coriander, parsley or radish. This meal is also very good for those using chopsticks – you don't need a knife to eat it.

(Serves 4)
800–900g sirloin steaks (2 cm thick if possible)
a little sunflower or vegetable oil for pan frying
15g finely chopped ginger
20–30g chopped myoga – if available
20–25g spring onions or chives – chopped
30g chopped celery
small bunch of shredded shiso leaves – or a mix
   of fresh basil and mint leaves
dashi shoyu sauce – to taste (see Ingredients Note)
grated daikon (mooli or Japanese white radish) –
   to taste

Ingredients Note:
To make dashi shoyu: Combine ¼ cup/50ml dashi
(fish stock) with ¼ cup/50ml soy sauce (half and
half) and add 1 tablespoon rice vinegar. Heat then
allow to cool before use.

1 Cut the steak into bite-size pieces.
2 Heat the oil in a frying pan and quickly cook the steak cubes, browning on all sides.
3 In a bowl combine the chopped vegetables (except the daikon).
4 When the steak is cooked to your liking, place on a serving dish and scatter the chopped vegetables on top.
5 Make the dashi shoyu sauce and pour it over the steak pieces. Eat accompanied by a small amount of the grated daikon.

Shabu Shabu Style Beef

This style of cuisine is called nabe ryori (casserole cooking) and is a very relaxing way to eat, sitting around a bubbling casserole dish, cooking at the table. In Japan we have restaurants that specialise in this one dish, serving only shabu shabu all year round. The ingredients are not only meat or fish but always include a variety of vegetables. After you've assembled the ingredients the cooking itself is simple and easy.

This dish is always cooked on a tabletop gas or electric ring. The cooking starts with the meat, then adding the tofu and finally the vegetables. Once we have eaten the meat and vegetables we add rice or noodles to the liquid, which by now is full of goodness and flavour. This nabe (casserole) style cuisine is great for dinner parties. As with many other recipes, we use a variety of sauces to dip the cooked meat vegetables or tofu into, and here I have included two.

(Serves 4)
For the stock:
2 sheets kombu seaweed about 10cm square
   to make the dashi stock
8 cups/1.6 litres water

80g dried kuzukiri (Japanese noodles –
   (see Ingredients Note)
300g soft/silken (1 pack)
200g of mizuna (a Japanese herb –
   (see Ingredients Note)
200g baby leeks
500g finely sliced beef
sesame dipping sauce
ponzu soy dipping sauce
300–400g ready cooked udon noodles

1 Wipe the kombu seaweed lightly to remove excess salt and then soak it in the water for 30 minutes.

2 In a separate pan boil a large quantity of water for the noodles. Cook over a moderate heat, following the instructions on the packet. Drain when cooked.

3 Drain and then wrap the tofu in kitchen paper to remove excess water, then cut into large bite size pieces.

4 Chop the mizuna into 7–8cm length pieces and slice the baby leeks diagonally into 2 cm thick pieces.

5 Arrange the beef, mizuna, baby leeks, cooked noodles and tofu attractively onto a large plate, keeping the different ingredients separate, as they will be cooked at different stages.

6 Prepare the sesame dipping sauce, the ponzu soy dipping sauce and condiments as described below.

7 Pour the soup stock into a casserole until ⅔ full and heat. Once it comes to the boil, turn down the heat and dip in the beef, slice by slice.

8 The beef will cook quickly so have a plate ready to put the cooked beef onto. Let everyone help themselves and dip the beef into the dipping sauces.

Ingredients Note:
Increasingly you can find kombu seaweed (kelp) in large supermarkets but if you cannot find it then make the initial 'soup' with fish stock seasoned with a little chicken stock.

The kuzukiri noodles are unique to Japan but I think you could substitute Thai glass noodles instead. The main thing is that you use noodles that do not have a strong flavour but have a lovely smooth texture. Mizuna is a green vegetable. I suggest that you use another green leafy vegetable like spinach or rocket, if you can't find mizuna locally.

Sesame Dipping Sauce

Sesame dipping sauce is essential for shabu shabu. This hand made sauce is very full-bodied and smells superb.

6 tablespoons sesame paste
2 tablespoons soy sauce
1 tablespoon rice vinegar
1 tablespoon caster sugar
1 teaspoon granulated chicken stock dissolved
    in ¼ cup/50ml hot water
coarsely ground sesame seeds – to taste

To make sesame sauce: In a bowl combine the sesame paste, soy sauce, vinegar, sugar and a mixture of hot chicken stock (making sure it's dissolved). Mix well. Add some ground sesame, if you like. I think it adds to the flavour.

For the ponzu soy dipping sauce: Make the ponzu sauce according to the recipe for Tofu and Ponzu soy sauce (page 81). To this add, according to your own taste; the juice from 4–5 sudachi or limes, 75g spring onions or chives, some grated daikon (mooli), some coarsely ground sesame seeds and chilli powder (shichimi togarashi).

9 Using a spoon, add the tofu to the casserole dish and bring the soup back to a gentle boil, then add the remaining vegetables and the cooked noodles. Add more stock if needed and, as it cooks, eat as before.

10 When the meat and vegetables are finished you can add the ready-cooked udon noodles (thick white Japanese noodles); they absorb the flavours of the enriched stock and are really delicious.

Sushi

All countries have their national dish – Japan's is sushi. It was originally created as a way of preserving fish but has subsequently become food that you eat on important occasions or when you have a special visitor. It is associated with fun and happy moments in life.

Its popularity is no longer limited to Japan. It seems to have captured the imagination of the world and now can be found outside Japan in many different places, including the sandwich sections of supermarkets.

I think that people are interested in the variety that sushi offers. It can be made into individual small balls of sushi rice with various toppings (nigiri style); it can be made into one large serving of sushi rice with various toppings (chirashi style); or it can be made into long rolls stuffed with different ingredients and then cut up into bite size pieces (maki style).

Nigiri zushi is considered to be best when it's created by professionals, who spend years training to cook the rice, slice the fish and put it all together. However, many Japanese households make chirashi zushi and maki zushi at home for parties and special occasions. I have created recipes for all types of sushi, nigiri, chirashi and maki, which can be easily replicated and don't require years of training.

Sushi

I have used many illustrations to show you how varied sushi can be. You can make individual balls with different toppings (nigiri zushi), you can make large bowls of rice with different toppings (chirashi zushi) or you can make long sushi rolls with different fillings which are cut into smaller rounds (maki zushi). It is a remarkably flexible dish.

One of the most important elements in sushi is the sushi rice itself, which is the usual Japanese short grain rice mixed with sweetened rice vinegar. You need to cook the rice with a little less water than usual as you will be adding the vinegar dressing while the rice is still warm and absorbent.

The best sushi rice is served when it is still ever so slightly warm, so avoid chilling it if possible. All references to rice in this chapter are to sushi rice; that is to say rice that has been dressed with sushi vinegar (you might like to note that sushi, as a word, becomes zushi after certain vowels.)

Sushi Vinegar Dressing:
Mix 1 cup/200ml rice vinegar with 3½ tablespoons of caster sugar in a small non-aluminium saucepan. Heat until the sugar has dissolved and then add 2 teaspoons of salt and ⅓ teaspoon of kombu cha powder, mix and allow to cool down. You can keep this in the fridge for 4–5 days before use. If you can't find the kombu cha powder then use a little more salt to taste.

320g uncooked rice and an equal amount of water by volume (makes 20–24 nigiri style small balls, 1 bowl of chirashi zushi, 4 maki roles or 6 ura maki rolls)

Sushi Rice:
Cook in the same way as regular rice (either in a rice cooker, microwave or saucepan). When cooked tip into a large shallow bowl or a wooden sushi pot and, while cooling, drizzle on 70–100ml of the sushi vinegar dressing (to taste) and fold in using a cutting and folding action – trying to make sure that you do not break the rice which would make it sticky. At the same time fan the rice to help speed the cooling process. When cool, use in your chosen sushi style.

Useful Ingredients

Even though sushi can be created in many different ways, there are certain ingredients which are always useful.

Wasabi I come from an area of Japan where wasabi is grown. It is only possible to grow wasabi in really clean, pure water. The root is grated and made into a paste – rather like a mustard. Wasabi is extensively used in sushi making – its fiery taste helps to cut through the rice's slight sweetness. Wasabi is now becoming more easily available internationally, though usually in a tube or in powdered form. It is definitely worth tracking down.

Nori We often use these crispy, shiny sheets of dried seaweed for sushi. It is a must for the maki style of sushi but it is also used chopped and sprinkled onto the chirashi style of sushi and with nigiri style. Sometimes we have 'roll your own' parties where we just put out all the ingredients and people make their own 'cones' of sushi (temaki zushi) using a sheet of nori as a wrap.

Shiso leaves These aromatic leaves are commonly served with sushi and with sashimi.

Gari This pickled ginger is always served with nigiri style sushi mainly to cleanse the palate in between servings. It is very simple to make. Take a piece of really fresh ginger (around 15g), peel, then slice very thinly with the grain. Sprinkle with a little salt and leave for 5–10 minutes, then put into boiling water to soften, and finally wash. Next soak it for 4 hours in a mix of 100ml sushi vinegar and 1 tablespoon of caster sugar. Drain off any excess liquid, pat dry and use as required.

Sesame seeds These are useful both to sprinkle on, or mix with, rice but are often used to roll 'inside out' maki zushi rolls in. They are sold in Japan already lightly toasted.

Suggested Toppings or Fillings

When you choose a topping think about what will bring the flavour to life – sometimes it needs a dab of wasabi, sometimes some grated ginger. As you become more familiar with the flavours, you will find what works well for you.

Sashimi   Raw fish. Most people associate sushi with raw fish – though it is not necessarily so. The easiest sashimi to work with is probably either tuna or salmon as neither of these fish are very strong tasting when raw. Almost any type of raw fish can be used, providing it is really fresh and that it is sliced in a way that makes it easy to eat. Ask your fishmonger for advice.

Cooked Fish   Traditionally, we do not use much cooked fish in sushi but king prawns are often used cooked. You can also use smoked fish, like smoked salmon or smoked eel.

Fish Roe   This can be used either as a main ingredient or as decoration.

Meat   I have included two illustrations using chicken. You can also use rare beef or even duck but make sure it is thinly sliced so it is easy to eat.

Omelette   A sweetened omelette provides not only taste but also an attractive colour. To make it, take three eggs, beat gently with a fork, add 1 tablespoon of sugar and a little salt. Cook as you would do with an ordinary omelette. You can then shred this for the chirashi zushi or cut it into strips for the nigiri or maki style of sushi. Adjust the thickness according to your own taste, although for the chirashi zushi the omlette must be very thin.

Vegetables   Many vegetables can be used with sushi, either cooked or raw. Most commonly used are cucumbers, avocados and chives.

Nigiri Style Sushi

Nigiri zushi is the type of sushi where a slice of fish, meat, omelette or vegetable is placed on a small ball of rice. Most people think this is the only type of sushi possible but, as you will see, it is not.

I often make these sushi rice balls using cling film to shape them – it is easier than doing it with your hands, especially if they are warm.

Tori, Kyuri no Nigiri Zushi

This has to be the easiest sushi in the world, using boiled breast of chicken, avocado and cucumber. Cut the chicken, avocado and cucumber into strips. Dab wasabi on each of the balls of rice, follow this with a strip of cucumber or avocado and then a piece of chicken. Put a little dressing on the chicken (2 tablespoons each of mirin and soy sauce combined with 2 teaspoons of caster sugar cooked for 2½ minutes in a microwave (600w) and then cooled) and wrap in nori seaweed.

Temari Zushi

For this sushi I have used egg topped with cod roe, white fish sashimi topped with grated ginger and spring onions, tuna sashimi and some cooked, sliced chicken (see recipe below)

250g boneless chicken thigh with skin
1 tablespoon mirin
1 tablespoon soy sauce
2 teaspoons caster sugar
Fry the chicken skin side down until brown and crispy, turn over and add the mirin, soy sauce and sugar. Fry until the chicken is cooked through. Take out and allow to cool before slicing thinly.

Oba Zushi

Oba is another name for shiso, so this sushi is called 'oba zushi'. I like to mix in a tablespoon of lightly toasted white sesame seeds into the sushi rice before making the balls. I then top these with thinly sliced sea bream dabbed with wasabi, ham with a dab of mayonnaise, smoked eel topped with some ground sansho or Szechuan pepper, or smoked salmon. On top of each piece of sushi I then place a shiso leaf. Ideally, I like to make these balls a little flat by placing them in a dish and pressing down with a plate to flatten them slightly. Serve with a little soy sauce and sudachi juice or lime juice. (I like to use the sea bream that has been marinated in kombu seaweed. See page 87, White Fish and Mozzarella Salad).

Chirashi Zushi

This is great for parties. Although it is better to use sushi rice for the recipe, it is possible to use long grain rice as it is served in a bowl or a large plate, and is not shaped in the way that nigiri zushi or maki zushi are. Here I used 150–200g cooked prawns, 200g smoked salmon, 200g sashimi-quality tuna, and 120g sashimi-quality white fish. Then I scattered some ribbons of sweetened omelette over and mixed in some shredded carrots cooked with sugar, soy sauce, and courgettes. Garnish it with salmon roe. You can use almost anything that you believe will work well together on this dish – both raw and cooked.

Maki Zushi

A rolling mat is a great help for this kind of sushi but if you cannot find one then you can use a similar sized square of greaseproof paper. Make sure you have all the ingredients ready to use before you start to construct the maki zushi. Use a sharp knife to cut it, and keep a bowl of water handy to wet the knife and your fingers, to stop the rice sticking. I find that 200g of sashimi-quality tuna is about right for 4 rolls, using 320g uncooked rice to 70ml sushi vinegar.

Maki Zushi

1 Take ½ a sheet of nori seaweed and place it on the rolling mat. Spread a thin layer of cooked rice evenly over the nori, leaving a centimetre of nori on each side free from rice as you will need this to seal the roll. Dab a little wasabi in a line across the rice – be careful not to use too much as it is very spicy.

2 Place the ingredients on the wasabi, but not too many or it won't roll well. For this roll use sashimi-quality tuna, roughly shredded shiso leaves and finely julienned cucumber.

3 Roll it carefully and evenly away from you, pressing it firmly. Remove the rolling mat, trim any ingredients that are protruding from the ends of the roll and cut into 2–3cm length pieces.

Ura Maki Zushi (inside out roll)

1 Place ½ a sheet of nori on the non-stick baking parchment and evenly spread a thin layer of fresh sushi rice across it (don't leave the edges free on this one). Carefully turn it over so the nori is facing upwards and add the ingredients. For this roll use crab sticks (200g approx), avocado and shiso leaves.

2 Use mayonnaise instead of wasabi, and dab on top of the ingredients. Roll carefully and evenly away from you.

3 Put some toasted sesame seeds on a plate and roll the sushi in them, so the roll is well coated.

4 Using a sharp knife, cut into 2–3cm length pieces and serve.

Vegetables

I want to encourage people to eat a lot of vegetables – you need them to create a balanced meal – but they don't have to be boring. In Japanese cuisine there are many ways of preparing vegetable dishes – raw, boiled, sautéed, simmered, pickled, dressed with a sesame sauce or simply grilled. However you prepare them, these dishes should be prepared with the same care and attention as you would give to the main dish – they are just as important and help to create a balance of colour, nutrition and taste.

One important feature of Japanese cooking is the emphasis it places on seasonality, and this is particularly applicable to vegetable dishes. Get to know which seasons are best for which vegetables in your country. For example, in Japan summer is associated with the best aubergines, cucumbers, tomatoes and pumpkins, whereas potatoes, cabbage, green beans and bamboo shoots are best eaten in spring. This may be different in the country where you live so it's worth finding out when particular vegetables are at their best. If you eat vegetables in season you will find an amazing improvement in flavour.

Although salads are not a part of traditional Japanese cuisine we have now heartily embraced the concept from overseas. In restaurants most western style meals come with a side salad, and Japanese supermarkets now sell a huge range of fresh vegetable produce.

A final point with vegetables is not to overcook them. Like the Italians and French, we like our vegetables 'al dente', so that we can appreciate and enjoy their natural flavour and texture.

Carrot & Tuna Salad

Everyone enjoys a salad, and this one can be served either as a starter or with a main course. Carrots are often used in stews and in non-Japanese dishes. This carrot recipe has proved to be one of my most popular. I think it is because carrots and tuna just work so well together. The other reason is that carrots are better if they are lightly cooked – even for a salad. I recommend using a microwave to cook the carrots as they leave the carrots still very crispy and tasty – difficult to achieve if you boil them.

(Serves 4)
200g carrots, peeled
90g tinned tuna
50g finely chopped onion
1 teaspoon chopped garlic
1 tablespoon sunflower or vegetable oil

Dressing:
2 tablespoons white wine vinegar
1 tablespoon mustard (preferably French
    grain mustard)
salt and pepper – to taste
soy sauce – to taste

1 First cut the carrots into lengths of 5–6 cm thin juliennes.
2 Put them into a bowl suitable for the microwave and mix in the onions, garlic and sunflower oil. Cover and microwave for 1–1½ minutes (600w).
3 Once the carrots are lightly cooked add the drained tuna and then the dressing and mix well.
4 Serve hot or cold.
5 Please note you can increase the amounts for this recipe , but when you microwave the carrots I find it is better to only do this amount at any one time.

Warm Aubergine Salad
Nasu no salad

Aubergines are very popular in Japan and often feature on restaurant menus or in home cooking in one delicious way or another. In fact, Japanese seasonings work very well with aubergines, especially sesame, as you will discover when you try this recipe.

(Serves 4)
350g aubergine

Sesame Sauce:
2 tablespoons sesame paste or tahini
    or unsweetened peanut butter
2½ tablespoons caster sugar
2 tablespoons soy sauce
1 tablespoon sake
1 tablespoon rice vinegar
2 tablespoons ground sesame seeds

20g myoga – if available – or chopped
    spring onions or shallots
5 shiso leaves or a mix of fresh mint
    and basil leaves

Ingredients Note:
Although myoga is sometimes called Japanese ginger it tastes nothing like ginger. So for this recipe I suggest you substitute spring onions or shallots. Japanese aubergines are smaller than those commonly found in Europe, so you may need to quarter the aubergines lengthways instead of halving them.

1 Chop off the aubergine stem and cut in half lengthways. Soak in water for around 5 minutes, then drain and wipe dry. Place the halved aubergines on kitchen paper on a microwave safe plate, cover and cook for 3–4 minutes (500w). Let stand for a few minutes. Divide into long strips and then squeeze to get rid of excess water.

2 To make the sauce: add the seasoning to the sesame paste in the order listed above and mix.

3 Slice the myoga (or shallots) finely, rinse and drain, then slice again in half. Cut the shiso leaves in half lengthways then into 5mm wide strips.

4 Place the aubergine on a dish and add the sauce, coating it well. Then scatter the myoga and shiso leaves on top.

Salad with Sesame Flavour Tofu Dressing

I like to use this sesame flavoured tofu sauce as an alternative to French dressing to liven up a plain salad. Because it's protein-rich, a salad dressed in this way can become a substantial part of a meal. The dressing works well on cooked or raw vegetables.

(Serves 4)
80g carrots
100g fresh green asparagus
50g mange tout
20–30g lettuce
sesame flavour tofu dressing (see below)
a handful of roughly ground sesame
seeds to garnish

1 Chop the carrots into 5cm matchsticks. Remove the woody part and any small outside leaves from the asparagus. Prepare the mange tout by removing any stringy edge, and top and tail if necessary.

2 Cook the three vegetables separately so they are just cooked but still retain their bite, and plunge immediately into ice-cold water for five minutes to chill. Drain well and dry on kitchen paper.

3 Cut the asparagus diagonally into 1cm wide pieces and each mange tout into 3 or 4 pieces. Tear the lettuce into fairly large pieces.

4 Combine all the vegetables in a bowl or on a deep plate and pour the sesame sauce over them. Sprinkle the ground sesame seeds on top.

(Serves 4)
300g soft/silken tofu (1 pack)
4 tablespoons sesame paste –
   or tahini or unsweetened peanut butter
1 tablespoon soy sauce
2 tablespoons caster sugar
2 tablespoons mirin
¼ cup/50ml dashi or fish stock
salt

Sesame Flavour Tofu Dressing

(Goma fumi tofu sauce)

1 Drain the tofu and wrap it in kitchen paper to remove excess water.

2 Mix the sesame paste, soy sauce, sugar, mirin and dashi stock together in a bowl. Break the tofu into small pieces with your hands and add to the bowl. Mix lightly and season with salt.

French Beans and Asparagus Chilli Style
Sayaingen to Asupara no Kinpira fu

I like using chilli in dishes like this and have found that it works very well with these particular vegetables. However, you can also try it with potatoes, carrots or anything you fancy. If you par boil the vegetables before you use them, it reduces their water content and keeps them crispy.

(Serves 4)
250g asparagus
200g French beans
2 tablespoons olive oil
2–3g finely chopped dried red chillis – to taste
3 tablespoons soy sauce

1 Chop off the woody part and strip any side leaves from the asparagus and top and tail the French beans. Cook them in boiling water until just cooked but still with a bite to them, then soak in chilled water.

2 When cooled, drain, then pat dry the beans and asparagus. Cut the asparagus into 3 and slice lengthways and cut the French beans into 2.

3 Heat the olive oil in a frying pan or a wok and lightly fry the vegetables. Add the chopped red chilli and soy sauce, quickly fry and serve.

Green Beans with Black Sesame Sauce

I am really happy when I have some good sesame seeds to cook with. I am also happy when I can use the natural colours of the ingredients to create an impact. The black sesame seeds used in this recipe make this simple dish quite striking.

(Serves 4)
200g green beans
50g roasted black sesame seeds
2 tablespoons caster sugar
½ tablespoon mirin
1 tablespoon soy sauce

1 String the beans and cut in half lengthways and then in half again. Par boil for a few minutes, taking care to remove before they soften. Drain and soak in iced water for a few minutes, drain again and pat dry.
2 In a mortar lightly crush the sesame seeds. Add the sugar, mirin and soy sauce and mix to a smooth paste.
3 Add the green beans into the mortar and toss, making sure that the beans are all well covered with the dressing. I think that it's better to mix the beans and sauce by hand for the best results.

Green Beans Mixed with Minced Meat
Ingen Hikiniku Itame

This dish with its sweet and spicy taste is perfect with rice. It's delicious even when served cold.

(Serves 4)
400g green beans
200g minced pork
3 tablespoons garlic and onion oil
   (see Ingredients Note)
2–3g red chilli peppers – finely sliced
   and de-seeded
3 tablespoons soy sauce
½ teaspoon caster sugar

Ingredients Note:
To make the garlic and onion oil: put 2 cloves of thinly sliced garlic, 200g thinly sliced onion, 100g finely chopped spring onion and 2 cups (400ml) of sunflower oil in a wok and heat on a low flame. When the spring onions turn dark brown remove from the heat. While the oil is still hot, filter using kitchen paper – taking care not to burn yourself. Leave it to cool. Make sure that the oil is cold before pouring into a bottle for future use. Please only use the oil while it still smells fresh.

1 String the green beans and cut diagonally into 3 pieces. Par boil for a few minutes, removing while still slightly firm. Soak in iced water and drain. Squeeze to remove any excess water.

2 Heat 1 tablespoon of the garlic and onion oil in a wok and fry the pork. Add the red chilli pepper and fry. Season with 2 tablespoons of soy sauce and the sugar.

3 Add a further 2 tablespoons garlic and onion oil and add the green beans and mix. Season quickly with a tablespoon of soy sauce and serve.

Spinach Ohitashi Style
Horenso no Ohitashi

Spinach prepared in this style is simple but unbelievably tasty.

(Serves 4)
300g fresh spinach
3 tablespoons roasted sesame seeds
nori seaweed – to taste
dried fish flakes – to taste
soy sauce – to taste

1 Par boil the spinach until just wilted but not cooked through.
Chill for a few minutes in iced water and then squeeze it well
to get rid of excess water. Chop into 3cm pieces.

2 Squeeze the spinach again then lightly separate out the leaves.

3 Divide into two piles and place on a serving plate. Crush the
seaweed into small flakes and sprinkle on one pile of spinach and
put the bonito dried fish flakes on the other. Add a little soy sauce.

Hijiki Seaweed Salad

I don't understand why so many westerners feel so nervous about eating seaweed – it's tasty, healthy and non-fattening. In Japanese cooking we use many types of seaweed but this is one of my favourites. Be careful not to over soak the hijiki seaweed and make it too soft. I have suggested using particular vegetables in this salad with the hijiki seaweed – these are ones I always have in my fridge. Use whatever type you have available.

(Serve 4)
10g hijiki seaweed (dried)
a variety of vegetables: lettuce, celery, carrots,
    cucumber and onions – to taste.

Anchovy Dressing:
10g anchovy fillets (tinned)
2 tablespoons sunflower or vegetable oil
1 tablespoon wine vinegar
a little caster sugar
pepper
1 teaspoon soy sauce

1 Soak the hijiki seaweed in warm water for about 10 minutes, drain well and dry. Cut it into short pieces if they are too long.
2 Cut the vegetables into thin strips, soak them in cold water for 5 minutes, drain and pat dry.
3 Mince the anchovy and mix it with the other ingredients for the dressing.
4 Mix the hijiki and cut vegetables and put on a serving dish. Pour over the anchovy dressing just before eating.

Desserts & Drinks

In the past, mostly we would finish a meal with some fresh fruit, but nowadays many Japanese enjoy something sweeter after eating, so serving desserts is now commonplace.

In fact I have always enjoyed serving dessert for my family, but never commercially made ones as I find them too sweet. Although many more homes than in the past now have an oven, many women still don't like using them, so I have developed dessert recipes that can be made without baking.

We have adopted many desserts from overseas and now regard many of them as being our own. Certainly, many looking at Japanese versions of cheesecake or tiramisu might find them quite altered, especially in the size of the serving. So, to keep to the spirit of Japanese cuisine, when you serve dessert serve less than you usually would – I think it should be just a taste rather than something that fills you up. Think small!

'Petal Style' Crepes

I think that many of my Japanese readers were surprised to find this recipe in my magazine. They always assumed that these traditional crepes are too difficult to make at home – until they tried this recipe. The crepe itself is a beautiful pale pink colour, created with a little food colouring. The filling is a sweet red bean paste which is a common ingredient in Japanese and Chinese desserts and is usually sold canned in Asian supermarkets. If you can't find it you can make your own quite simply – see my note below. Sweet things like this are always served with Japanese green tea or Chinese jasmine tea.

(For 10 crepes)
100g plain flour
1 cup/200ml water
1 teaspoon sugar
salt
sunflower or vegetable oil
a few drops of red food colouring
a little water
200g sweetened ready-prepared bean paste.

Ingredients Note:
If you can't find bean paste you can easily make it yourself. Soak azuki beans overnight and then cook until soft, then mash. Add sugar to taste and stir vigorously over a low heat until the sugar has dissolved.

1 Put the flour, water, sugar and salt into a bowl and whisk well until smooth, then add a teaspoon of sunflower oil.

2 Mix a few drops of the food colouring with a little water, and add to the batter little by little, until it turns a pale cherry blossomcolour (be careful not to use too much colouring – you don't want a lurid pink.) Leave to stand for 30 minutes.

3 Heat a spoonful of oil in a frying pan on a low heat so the surface is well oiled, then gently wipe off any excess with kitchen paper. Pour in enough batter to make a thin crepe of 10–12cm in diameter, tilting the pan to ensure that it is even. Leave the crepe to cook on one side, then turn over and cook briefly. Repeat as before until you have used all the batter. Leave the pancakes to cool.

4 Take a dessertspoonful of the bean paste (around 20g), shape into a ball and place in the centre of each crepe. Fold in half, then fold again as in the photo.

5 The best way to serve these crepes is to place a couple on a small dish for each person – if possible find one that complements the pink colour.

Steamed Cream Cheese Muffins

This recipe is so simple that you can easily make these muffins for breakfast in the morning. As they are light and sweet they are also good for afternoon tea.

(Serves 4)
40g cream cheese
½ tablespoon white wine
1 tablespoon double cream
1 tablespoon sunflower or vegetable oil
vanilla essence – to taste
2 medium size eggs
50g granulated sugar
50g plain flour
½ teaspoon baking powder

Possible fillings:
Butter cream
Mix 3 tablespoons of caster sugar with 50g of softened, unsalted butter until it becomes pale. Slowly add 3 tablespoons of double cream mixing as you go.

Peanut Cream
Add 2 tablespoons caster sugar to 6 tablespoons of double cream. Whisk for 5–6 minutes until thick and add 4 tablespoons of peanut butter (crunchy type). Mix well.

To make the cream cheese mixture:

1 First prepare the dishes: line 4 large ramekin dishes (9 × 5cm) with greaseproof paper. You can either cut pieces to size, or simply press paper into the dish to create a creased paper effect.

2 Put the cream cheese and white wine in a heat-resistant container and cover. Microwave for 20 seconds (500w).

3 Take out and whisk until it becomes creamy.

4 Add the double cream, sunflower oil and vanilla essence. Mix well.

5 In a separate bowl beat the eggs and add the sugar. Whisk until it thickens.

6 Add the flour and baking powder to the egg and sugar mixture, mixing lightly and then add the cream cheese.

7 Half fill each ramekin dish with batter and cover loosely with cling film, allowing plenty of room for the mixture to rise.

8 Microwave on a low heat for 5 minutes (150–200w) before turning it up to a higher heat and microwaving for a further 1½ minutes (500w).

9 Turn the muffins out while they are still hot and remove the greaseproof paper.

Mont Blanc Style Dessert

The 'Mont Blanc' style of cakes is very popular in Japan and these mountain shaped cakes can be found in most cake shops. They are usually made from cooked, puréed chestnuts, but I think that they are just as good made with sweet potato.

The important point is that the little mound of purée is decorated with more purée which has been put through a potato ricer or mincer, to create thick shreds or ribbons – the end result should look a little like that famous mountain!

(Serves 4)
300g sweet potato
3–4 tablespoons sugar
14g butter
1 beaten egg yolk
60–70ml double cream
1 tablespoon rum
1 teaspoon mirin
cinnamon powder – to taste
icing sugar – to taste

1 Peel the sweet potato and cut into pieces just slightly bigger than bite size. As you cut, drop them immediately into a bowl of water to prevent them discolouring. When ready to cook, drain the pieces and pat them dry.

2 Put some kitchen paper in a microwave resistant bowl and add the sweet potato. Cover and place in a microwave for 5–6 minutes (500w).

3 Remove from the microwave, take off the cling film and mash. Add the sugar, butter and half the egg yolk (you will need the other half later) and mix well. Leave the mixture to cool.

4 In a separate bowl, lightly whisk the cream. Fold the whisked cream into the mashed potatoes then add the rum and mix again.

5 The mixture should now be quite stiff and easy to handle. Take half of the mix and make eight egg-shaped portions. Place on a baking tray and glaze with a mixture made of the remaining half egg yolk and the teaspoon of mirin.

6 Place under a medium hot grill until they turn golden brown. Leave to cool.

7 Place two portions per person on individual plates.

8 Finally, take the remaining half of the mixture and put it in a potato ricer. Squeeze potato shreds over each portion, dividing it equally. Sprinkle each 'mountain' with the cinnamon powder and icing sugar.

Watermelon Sorbet
Suika no Sherbert

Watermelon is a wonderful fruit. It feeds the senses with its green shell, red flesh and black seeds. It is also fantastic on a hot summer's day when its watery and crispy flesh is just what you need to refresh yourself. However, I think this sorbet is even more refreshing than the original fruit.

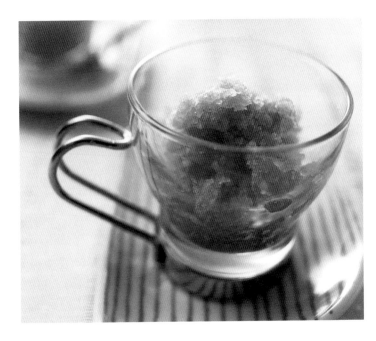

(Serves 5~6)
3 tablespoons sugar
3 tablespoons water
1kg watermelon flesh
1 tablespoon lemon juice
1 tablespoon Kirsch liquor

1 Mix together the sugar and water in a heat resistant container. Put in a microwave and cook for 3 minutes (500w) without covering. Leave to cool.
2 Take the watermelon pulp and remove the seeds then mash the pulp with a balloon whisk. Add the cooled syrup, lemon juice and Kirsch to taste and mix well.
3 Pour into a stainless steel square mould and cover with cling film. Freeze for a couple of hours.
4 To serve, scrape the sorbet into icy granules with a spoon, and serve in a dish that shows off the beautiful colour.

Green Tea Jelly
Macha Jelly

Once you eat this pudding, you will become addicted to it. This is a 'must have' Japanese dessert! The slightly bitter taste of the green tea powder and the condensed milk are a perfect combination. I love making this jelly so that it only just sets so don't be surprised at how soft it is.

(Serves 4)
The Jelly:
5g powdered gelatine
1⅓ tablespoons green tea powder (macha powder)
4 tablespoons caster sugar
¼ cup/50ml boiling water
1½ cup/300ml tap water

The Milk Sauce:
½ cup/100ml condensed milk
½ cup/100ml milk

some sweetened red azuki beans – to taste

Ingredients Note:
You can buy tins of red azuki beans in most Asian food shops. (see page 149 Petal Style Crepes)

1 Put 1½ tablespoons of water in a heat-resistant bowl and add the powdered gelatine and mix well. Cover and microwave (500w) for 10 seconds until the gelatine has fully dissolved.

2 In a separate bowl mix the green tea powder and sugar.
Add the hot water little by little to make a paste.
Then add a further 1½ cups/300ml of tap water and mix well.

3 Add the gelatine liquid to the tea and mix it in quickly. Pour into a mould and put in the fridge to set stirring occasionally to prevent the mixture separating.

4 To make the milk sauce, combine 100ml of condensed milk and 100ml of milk. Once the jelly has set scoop out and serve using a large spoon. Pour over the milk sauce and top with azuki beans to taste.

Tea

It is amazing how Japanese green tea has taken the world by storm. Not so long ago it would be inconceivable to think that you could find it in most supermarkets internationally. Now you can find green tea bags almost everywhere and the health benefits from drinking the tea are well recognised.

Green tea (o-cha) is taken all day in Japan. It is impossible to have a meal without it. In restaurants your teacup is constantly topped up, at no extra cost. In hotel rooms, you will always find a kettle and green tea. At any meeting you will automatically be presented with a cup of tea. Tea is everywhere!

Outside of Japan it's probably easier to find tea bags than loose tea, but most Japanese, including me, prefer the taste of tea made with fresh tea leaves. I come from one of the major tea growing areas of Japan, Shizuoka Prefecture, and I cannot imagine using anything other than good, fresh green tea leaves. If you can find loose tea then try it in preference to bags.

O-cha is easy to make, providing you follow a few simple rules.

1 Heat the teapot before putting the tea leaves in.

2 Don't use boiling water – the water should be around 50–70c.

3 Japanese teapots are small and you should use around 2–3 teaspoons of tea per pot. Do not leave the tea for more than 2–3 minutes before pouring.

4 Pour the tea little by little into the cups so each cup has an equivalent colour and taste.

5 Use the best tea you can afford. You can use the leaves again – use hotter water for the second and third use.

Our tea cups are quite small and without handles so be careful not to fill the cup too much or you will not be able to hold it until it has cooled down. A traditional style of cup comes in pairs – a large one for the man, and a smaller one for the woman. I have designed a modern version – a pair of cups of equal size. We have a wonderful range of cups and teapots, from fine china to chunky earthenware, and it's always fun deciding on which style to use.

Hojicha is most commonly drunk after meals. This tea has a wonderful nutty flavour as a result of the tea leaves being roasted. Although hojicha is more difficult to find than green tea you can easily make you own.

Take a handful of green tea leaves and put them in a wok or a frying pan and cook on a low heat, shaking from time to time. When the leaves change colour, it's ready for use.

Iced green tea is a popular drink in summer. I love iced green tea. To make it, make the tea slightly stronger than usual. Make enough pots of tea to fill a jug, allow to cool, then add lots of ice cubes. Try it out on your friends and family during the summer.

Glossary

If you want to ask for things in Japanese (in a shop or restaurant) it is an easy language to pronounce as long as you remember to pronounce each letter individually and to keep the vowels pure: 'ʌ' as in apple, 'ɪ' as in ink, 'ʊ' as in put, 'ɛ' as in egg and 'ɔ' as in pot. It is not accented and in the main no sound is lengthened more than others.

Daikon

Daikon

Ginger

Katsuo bushi

Shaved katsuo bushi

Ao-nori Dried, finely chopped seaweed. Often used on top of okonomiyaki.

Asari clams A small type of clam, common to Japan.

Bento Japanese lunch box.

Chirimen Zansho Dried baby anchovies flavoured with sweet soy sauce and sansho pepper.

Daikon Japanese radish, sometimes found in Asian shops called mooli.

Dashi Stock made from kombu and dried fish flakes (katsuo bushi). The basis of much of Japanese cooking.

Dashi no moto Instant dashi granules, available in Japanese stores.

Ginger Fresh ginger comes as a knobbly root vegetable that needs to be peeled before use. It is frequently used in Japanese cooking, both fresh and pickled. There are two types of pickled ginger – the thin wafer thin slices eaten with sushi, (gari) and the red julienned versioned that is eaten with okonomiyaki and yakisoba (beni-shoga).

Harusame noodles Very fine translucent noodles made from mung bean starch, or more likely sweet potato or potato starch. The name means 'spring rain' which they resemble.

Ichimi Togarashi Chilli powder.

Katsuo Bushi Smoked and dried bonito fish that is shaved into very fine flakes before use. Used in many recipes, including dashi, it has a distinctive flavour.

Kinome The young leaves of the sansho plant. Not readily available in the west.

Kombu Kelp seaweed. Used to make dashi stock and in simmered foods.

Kombu cha powder Ground kombu used as a tea. It has a good strong salty flavour.

La Yu Chilli oil, often used with Chinese dishes like gyoza.

Mentaiko The roe of the Alaska Pollack or cod, salted and seasoned with chilli pepper.

Mentsuyu A basic dipping sauce, usually made from dashi, soy sauce, salt and sugar.

Mirin A sweet alcoholic liquid used in cooking to tenderise and sweeten, and balance saltiness. An essential ingredient in Japanese cooking.

Miso A rich savoury paste made from fermented soy beans, salt and grain (usually rice or barley). It keeps for years and is a protein rich addition to many dishes. It's the essential ingredient in miso soup. Red miso (akamiso) is dark and high in protein and salt. White miso (shiromiso) is milder and sweeter and suitable for dressings. Medium (awase miso) is all-purpose, being a mix of red and white miso.

Mitsuba Its botanical name is Cryptotaenia japonica and it resembles flat leaf parsley in appearance but not taste, being more aromatic and fragrant. Dried leaves are available.

Mizuna Brassica campestris. A leafy green, sometimes called pot-herb mustard.

Mushrooms Japan has a huge variety of mushrooms, many of which you cannot find overseas. Most commonly used is the shiitake (dark and round – a little like chestnut mushrooms). However, maitake, shimeji, eringi and enoki are all commonly used: they are usually available in clumps and differ mainly in colour and thickness of the stalks.

Myoga The fragrant bud of a type of ginger plant, Zingiber mioga. Available pickled, but occasionally you can find the fresh bud in oriental stores. Ginger is not a substitute.

Kombu

Myoga

Negi

Negi

Sashimi

Negi Japan has a huge range of vegetables from the onion family. Naga negi and banno negi are the most common and are comparable to our spring onions and leeks.

Nori Seaweed, most usually encountered as dried thin crisp sheets which are used to wrap around sushi.

Nira Garlic chives – very pungent and tasty.

Pak Choy Sometimes spelt as pak choi or bak choi. A Chinese leafy green vegetable.

Ponzu Soy Sauce A dipping sauce made from soy sauce and citrus juice, traditionally sudachi or yuzu, but nowadays also lemon.

Potato starch (katakuriko) Similar to cornflour but stronger, so use a little more cornflour if you cannot find potato starch.

Rice (kome) The technical name for Japanese rice is Oryza sativa japonica. It is short grained so sticks together and can be eaten with chopsticks.

Rice vinegar This commonly used vinegar is made from rice and is low in acidity and mild in flavour.

Sansho pepper Made from the ground seedpods of the prickly ash, slightly spicy with a hint of citrus. Sansho is closely related to Szechwan pepper, which is acceptable as a substitute.

Sake Japanese rice wine. Used to tenderise foods. Similar to a very dry sherry. Can be drunk hot or cold.

Sashimi Sliced fish that is eaten raw, so must be extremely fresh.

Sesame oil Toasted sesame oil has a strong flavour and is used in small amounts. It burns easily.

Sesame paste Japanese sesame paste is rich and smooth being made from toasted sesame seeds. Tahini is an acceptable alternative, although less refined.

Sesame seeds In Japan sesame seeds are usually sold already toasted. Both black and white sesame seeds are available.

Shichimi Togarashi This is a frequently used mix of seven spices, including chilli.

Shiso Sometimes known as perilla or beefsteak plant and part of the mint family. Its leaves look rather like nettle leaves and are very aromatic. It is used as a garnish with sashimi, or chopped and served with rice or in salads.

Shochu A colourless spirit distilled from grain or starch, such as potato, barley or millet.

Shokoshu A Chinese rice wine that has a stronger flavour than sake with a subtle undertone of herbs.

Somen Very fine white wheat noodles, usually eaten chilled in summer.

Soy sauce Made from soybeans, wheat and salt, soy sauce is the ubiquitous flavouring in Japanese cooking. The regular soy sauce (koikuchi) is readily available in the west. A thinner soy sauce (usukuchi) is lighter, but actually saltier, and used when you don't want to darken the appearance of the food too much.

Tarako Salted cod roe.

Tentsuyu Dipping sauce for tempura – it's a diluted version of mentsuyu, diluted with dashi and served hot.

To-Ban-Jan Chinese chilli paste.

Tofu A curd made from co-agulated soy milk. There are two main types of fresh tofu: soft or silken tofu (kinugoshidofu). This falls apart easily and is best eaten just as it is with soy sauce and ginger, but it's also good for dips and dressings. Firm or cotton tofu (momendofu) is the pressed curds and therefore firmer. This is good for cooking.

Wakame A mild and delicate seaweed. Available dried it quickly re-hydrates and is a common addition to miso soup, and salads.

Wasabi The ground root of what is often referred to as 'Japanese horseradish'. This is the green paste served with sashimi and sushi. Extremely pungent it can be bought in tubes, or as a powder ready to mix with water.

Yuzu A Japanese citrus fruit used in many recipes.

Zaa Sai Chinese pickles – green, crunchy and nutty in flavour, which need to be rinsed of salt before using.

Japanese food shops in the UK

Akaneya Japanese Food Shop
272 Hyde End Road, Reading, RG7 1DL
t: 0118 988 4616
e: akaneya@orbix.uk.nwt

Arigato Japanese Supermarket
48–50 Brewer Street, Piccadilly, London W1
t: 020 7287 1722
f: 020 7287 7579
(This store will accept orders by fax and send
anywhere in the UK by post)

Atari-ya (Finchley)
595 High Road, North Finchley, London N12 0DY
t: 020 8446 6669

Atari-ya (West Acton)
7 Station Parade, Noel Road, London W3 0DS
t: 020 8896 1552
e: info@atariya.co.uk

Atari-ya (Golders Green)
15–16 Monkville Parade,
Finchley Road, London NW11 0AL
t: 020 8896 1552

Cardiff Food
116 Woodville Road, Cathays, Cardiff CF24 4EE
t: 02920 223 225

Heisei Mart
15–16 Monkville Parade, Temple Fortune,
Finchley Road, London NW11 0AL
t: 020 8455 6500
e: info@heiseimart.co.uk
www.heiseimart.co.uk

Japan Centre Food Shop
Japan Centre 212 Piccadilly, London W1J 9HG
t: 020 7434 4218
www.japancentre.com

Jasmin
c/o Stanton House Hotel, The Avenue,
Stanton Fitzwarren, Swindon, Wilts. SN6 7SD
t: 01793 861 777
(Some dried foodstuffs, open Weds, Fri and Sun)

Minamoto Kitchoan (Japanese sweets only)
44 Piccadilly, Piccadilly Circus, London W1J 0DS
t: 020 7437 3135

Miura Foods
44 Coombe Road, Kingston-upon-Thames,
Surrey KT2 7AF
t: 020 8549 8076

Oriental City Super Market
399 Edgware Road, London NW9 0JJ
t: 020 8200 0009

Rice Wine Shop
82 Brewer Street, London W1F 9VA
t: 020 7439 3705
e: info@ricewineshop.com
www.ricewineshop.com

TK Trading Japanese Foods
Unit 6–7, The Chase Centre, Chase Road,
Park Royal, London NW10 6QD
t: 020 8453 1743
www.japan-foods.co.uk

Yamazaki Bakery
Unit A18 Oriental City,
399 Edgware Road, London NW9 0JJ
t: 020 8205 5569
e: 011td@msn.com

Yoshino & Co.(UK) Ltd.
(Delicatessen Yoshino)
Japan Centre Basement, 212 Piccadilly,
London W1J 9HH
t: 020 7434 3610